MAINTENANCE ARCHITECTURE

MAINTENANCE ARCHITECTURE
HILARY SAMPLE

THE MIT PRESS
CAMBRIDGE, MASSACHUSETTS
LONDON, ENGLAND

This book was set in PF DIN Pro by The MIT Press. Printed and bound in Canada.

Cover image design and concept by Vanessa van Dam (Amsterdam).

Library of Congress Cataloging-in-Publication Data
Names: Sample, Hilary, author.
Title: Maintenance architecture / Hilary Sample.
Description: Cambridge, MA : The MIT Press, 2016. | Includes bibliographical
    references and index.
Identifiers: LCCN 2016005967 | ISBN 9780262034975 (hardcover : alk. paper)
Subjects: LCSH: Architecture—Human factors. |
    Buildings—Maintenance—Miscellanea.
Classification: LCC NA2542.4 .S26 2016 | DDC 720.28/8—dc23 LC record
    available at http://lccn.loc.gov/2016005967ISBN: 978-0-262-03497-5

10 9 8 7 6 5 4 3 2 1

Contents

3

VISUALIZING DECAY

4

MODERNIZING MAINTENANCE

5
POST-OCCUPANCY AND ALTERNATE ARCHITECTURAL FUTURES

Acknowledgments

This book began as a series of unexpected observations in two different settings. It has evolved over a period of time, and exists alongside many other projects. I hope it will read not like a typical book but an extension of past and present projects, buildings, ideas, videos, writings, and thinking about architecture's place in the world. It's a product of the repetition of disparate themes—maintenance and architecture, and their undeniable intersection. In January 2000, traveling between Princeton, New Jersey, and Rotterdam, the Netherlands, I first took note of two artworks, Iñigo Manglano-Ovalle's *Le Baiser/The Kiss* and Jeff Wall's *Morning Cleaning*. Both were photographs, and each presented specific acts of domestic cleaning of modern iconic architecture. The juxtaposition of the mundane—cleanliness—against the extraordinary—architecture—upended an entrenched understanding of modernism's fixity as illustrated in books and journals. These specific photographs seemed taboo, corrupting the ideal that architecture should have a fixed representation. Each rendered the image of architecture as overtly social and political, trumping aesthetics and architectural history. Or so it seemed. I could not forget them, and my collection soon grew by two more images, Job Koelewijn's *Cleaning the Rietveld Pavilion* and Rem Koolhaas's *Cleaning the Barcelona Pavilion* (reproduced here as figure 0.4). More images followed from there, with scribbled extended captions, and several articles have been published, written in between undertaking real building projects, starting an office, and so on.

In 2004, I wrote about maintenance first as a short essay in *Praxis: Journal of Building + Writing*, for which I have to thank the editors Ashley Schafer, Amanda Reeser, Irina Verona, and Jeannie Kim for their support and valuable suggestions. The more I looked into the subject of maintenance, the more it became entangled. The social and political could not, in fact, be distilled from the aesthetic and the formal-technological; all are deeply woven into this history. Maintenance as a subject is messy. I am sympathetic to maintenance because I don't believe architecture's autonomous practice can exist without an indebtedness to it, as much as I also am wary about making such a statement. I want to believe in the art of architecture beyond science, beyond technology, but there are moments when it is necessary to acknowledge that architecture is architecture only because of certain things, acts, and thinking. In a fair world, maintenance would not exist.

In the past, celebrated architects completed works related to health, and it isn't surprising that some of those same architects (as the works shown in this book demonstrate) frequently thought of and represented maintenance by extension. Other writers, theorists, and historians have also touched on maintenance. One such was Reyner Banham, and I'd like to thank the University of Buffalo School of Architecture and Planning for the opportunity to teach as the Reyner Banham Chair, which presented the opportunity to examine Banham's work, especially *The Architecture of the Well-Tempered Environment*, which led to the addition of a fourth image of the Lever House. I want to thank Mehrdad Hadighi and Kent Kleinman for the opportunity to hold this significant teaching fellowship, Dean Brian Carter for his support at that time and since, and Annette Le Cruyer for conversations about technologies, façades, materials, and metals. The collection of images grew larger, by then maybe more than a passing curiosity, and a MacDowell Colony Fellowship gave me time and space to rethink ideas of endurance and maintenance and their intersection with architecture and the city. Later, at the Canadian Centre for Architecture, conversations with Caroline Maniaque, Lucia Allais, Lydia Kallipoliti, and Reinhold Martin influenced the scope and refined the content of this research. I want to thank Phyllis Lambert and Mirko Zardini for their willingness to grant me access to the CCA collections and community; Giovanna Borasi and Steffen Boddeker provided further intellectual conversations and support. I'd especially like to thank the CCA librarians, and Peter Sealy for his research assistance.

In academia I've had numerous conversations with and support from colleagues, and would especially like to thank Beatriz Colomina for initially supporting this project through an independent study at Princeton and in a text in the *Journal of the Society of Architectural Historians*, as well as Keller Easterling, Mark Wigley, Jorge Otero-Pailos, David Gissen, Vanessa van Dam, Amale Andraos, Eric Howeler, and

Kiel Moe. Michelle Addington assisted in developing the early stages of the book, and Mary McLeod offered encouraging advice and insightful suggestions on scholarship throughout the process of writing it.

Most recently "Towers, Maintenance, and the Desire for Effortless Permanence" has appeared in the volume *Sustain and Develop* in the series 306090, published by Princeton Architectural Press; "Protocols and Contingencies" in the *Journal of the Society of Architectural Historians* Media Reviews; and "Glass Acts" in *Log*, edited by Cynthia Davidson. I'd like to thank *Log*, *Praxis*, 306090, and *JSAH* for granting me permission to reproduce images and text here.

I'd also like to thank Gina Morrow, Meredith McDaniel, Ivi Diamantopoulou, Paul Ruppert, Michaela Friedberg, Matt Zych, Bryan Norwood, Sara Stevens, and Esther Choi for their careful readings of the text, which owes much to them.

Essential materials were made available by the following people: Nicolette A. Dobrowolski from the Syracuse University Special Collections Research Center William Lescaze Archive; Robert Carlucci, of the Visual Resource Collection, Holly Hatheway, Assistant Director for Collections, and Carolyn Caizzi, Technology Specialist, from the Robert B. Haas Family Arts Library, Yale University; and Kraig Binkowski, Chief Librarian, Reference Library and Archives, Yale Center for British Art. Thanks for assistance with image collections to Francesca Picchi of *Domus*, Elizabeth Kurbany and Emma Bird from SOM, Evan Lee at Jeff Wall's studio, Gini O'Neal at the Tuxedo Park Library, and Louise Lemoine of Living Architectures. At Columbia University's Avery Library, thanks to Janet Parks, Nicole Richards, and Carole Ann Fabian. A special thank you to each of the contributors for sharing their work.

I'd like especially to thank Roger Conover at the MIT Press for his encouragement and commitment, and his colleagues Matthew Abbate, Margarita Encomienda, Victoria Hindley, Gillian Beaumont, Justin Kehoe, Jim Mitchell, and David Weininger.

And lastly, thanks to my family and especially Michael Meredith.

Hilary Sample
New York

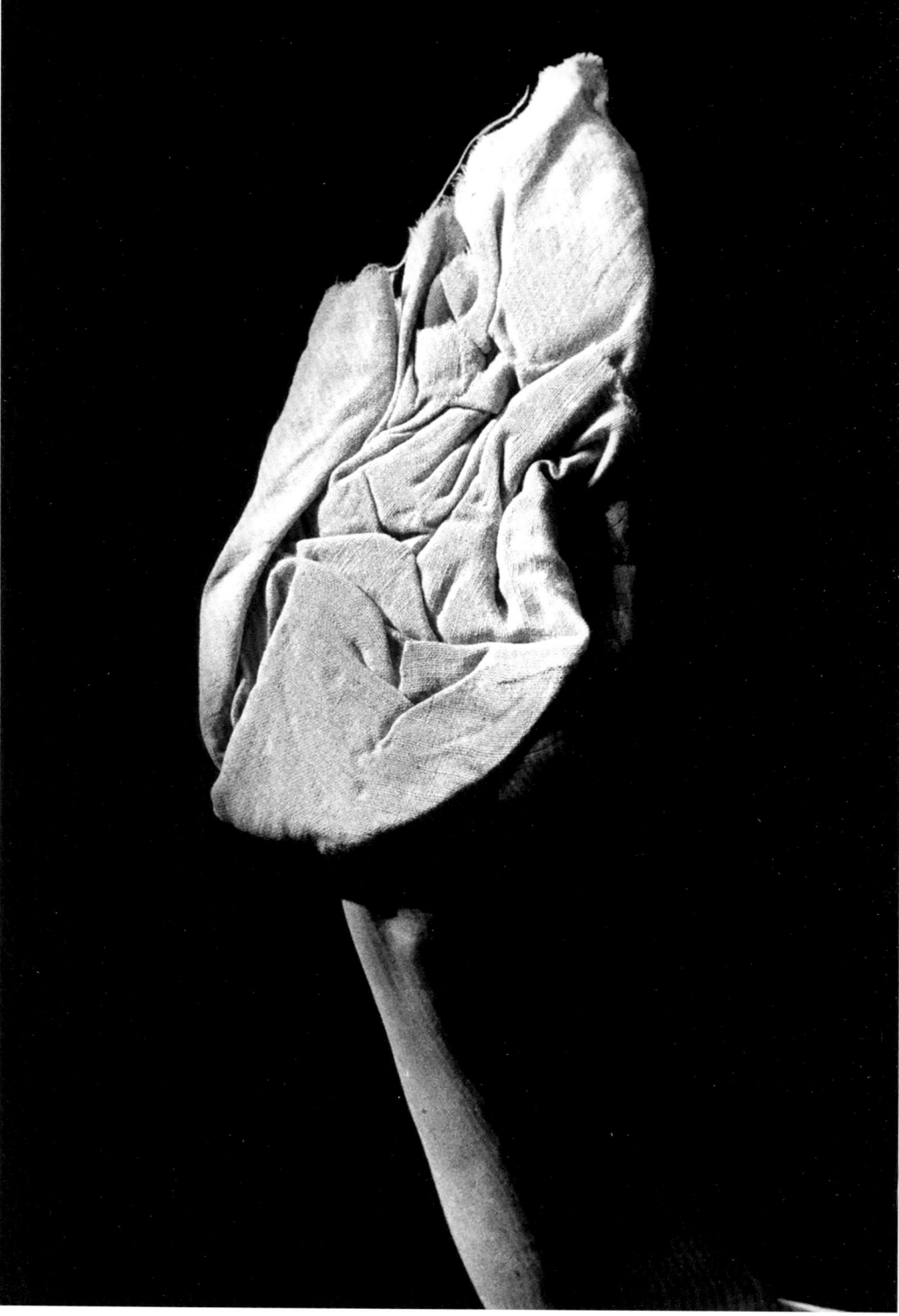

Introduction

Previously built architecture is a maintenance issue
more than anything else.
Gordon Matta-Clark[1]

Maintenance plays a crucial role in the production of architecture, yet by and large architects have treated it with indifference. Despite its existence everywhere, the history of maintenance has been neglected as part of the discourse from within architecture.[2] Dismissed as irrelevant to form making and design, maintenance has been cast aside, appearing (if at all) in the back-section advertisements of architecture magazines or categorized as a problem to be undertaken after construction, not treated as a disciplinary concern or as having any relevance to the production of an art form.[3] Perhaps this is because buildings deteriorate slowly and imperceptibly, but this disciplinary disaffection is undeserved. With the day-to-day wear and tear on surfaces, buildings eventually decay if left unkept. Labor is required through the form of maintenance to keep buildings looking new. But maintenance is more than labor; it is a result of work performed by architects in their making of buildings. Following the philosopher Hannah Arendt's distinction between labor and work, looking at maintenance offers a new representation on work or a "lasting thing."[4] And now more than ever it is time to pay attention to it, as our contemporary architecture culture values images of those things that are new or appear to be new rather than lived in, and privileges a work of art in its original form. Understanding the complexities required for an image to endure is not abstract, and not about labor alone. While architecture has turned a blind eye to the subject of maintenance, others have made it the object

0.1

Ralph Gibson, *Window Washer, Paris*, 1975. Gift of Francis Farr. Image courtesy of the Yale University Art Gallery.

of their work, primarily through art, revealing new realities and subjectivities that architecture should revisit.

By making maintenance the subject of their work, artists reveal that, in the postmodern split between art and life, maintenance was cast on the side of life and technology—within architecture, especially, forgotten and removed from primary imagery, and when it *was* introduced, rendered as a technical act performed without consequences for the creative act of design. Yet maintenance is needed if beauty is to endure. It is labor. But it can be argued that it both produces work and affects the production of work. This portrayal of maintenance emphasizes its routine qualities and the endless repetition of skilled labor it requires. Maintenance, unlike general cleaning, should not be categorized as part of what Arendt called "reproductive" labor—manual acts of unskilled labor.[5] Maintenance should be understood as labor, but skilled labor, especially when it involves large-scale buildings like towers. Meanwhile, buildings require labor and work if they are to be considered imageworthy, a goal in which maintenance plays an inherent part. In modernism, architects thought through the problem of maintenance as part of the architecture, and the division between art and life did not yet exist. It is time to rethink the relevance of maintenance's effects on contemporary architectural practice, image production, representation, and culture at large.

Artists, on the contrary, have continued to challenge our notions of endurance and permanence in response to modernism and neo-avant-garde approaches toward art and work. As early as the 1960s and 1970s, people like Mierle Laderman Ukeles and Gordon Matta-Clark brought issues of maintenance and spectacle to the fore in projects like, respectively, "Manifesto for Maintenance Art" (1969) and *Conical Intersect* (1975). This book examines a range of art practices—historical and contemporary—in order to address the problem of maintenance from an architectural perspective, and speculates how expanded thinking on the subject could impact future design and discourse. When a careful look is taken at the intersection between art, architecture, and maintenance, the recursive problems of subjects and objects surface in interesting ways.

Maintenance originates as a modern concern, though unlike clean-ing, its more domestic counterpart, it is not a "happening," as in the kinds of spontaneous events the artist Allan Kaprow created. But con-temporary artists have recast it as a "happening" through their works, repositioning the subject as "cool." While maintenance is not the origin of architecture, in architecture it is possible to find an origin of mainte-nance. Thinking back to projects such as Buckminster Fuller's Dymaxion House (1929) or SOM's Lever House (1952), it is clear that issues of upkeep at both the domestic and urban scales were coming to the fore by the mid-twentieth century. Maintenance as a subject aligns itself with philosopher Martin Heidegger's reading of *Dasein*'s experiences regarding tools, things of nature, and other human beings as being-in-the-world.[6] Through a careful reading of archival building photographs and architectural drawings, maintenance's history can be found.

Not until the early twentieth century did photography become a widely accepted mode of architectural representation in magazines, newspapers, books, and elsewhere. Photographs became *the* way to circulate images of buildings to wide audiences, while simultaneously bringing problems of iconography and imageability to the discipline. Maintenance is a subject that appears and reappears throughout mod-ern and contemporary histories of architecture, but also in contempo-rary art. It is impossible to do without maintenance unless the desired outcome is decay or death. Through images of maintenance, both in architecture and in art, it is possible to see the various roles that it plays.

This book is primarily concerned with a few specific types of build-ings—the private house, pavilions, and high-rise buildings—and, because of the significance of images in the modern period, it pays particular attention to buildings constructed with novel and developing materials, technologies, and precise detailing. This includes modern buildings like Lever House (1952) and the U.S. Steel Building (1971), and contemporary buildings like the Beijing Water Cube (2008) and the Netherlands Embassy in Berlin (2004). The architects Alison and Peter Smithson present an imperative to assess this kind of work in their "Prelude" to *The Heroic Period of Modern Architecture*:

One further thought. No one has properly observed a quite definite special sub-category of modern architecture. An architecture of the enjoyment of luxury materials, of the well-made, of the high finish. It is special to Mies and occasional to Le Corbusier and Gropius.[7]

Taking the Smithsons' prompt, *Maintenance Architecture* examines buildings in this special subcategory, citing a range of modern and contemporary works that take on maintenance as a subject without "one-thingly character."[8] Maintenance is deeply connected to issues of imageability and architecture's present-day concerns. It is more than a problem of trying to be or appear eternally new. Maintenance presents evidence of nature, evidence of human relationships beyond the technical.[9]

The evolution of building construction methods, in conjunction with the increasing prevalence of architectural photography, began to produce a kind of architecture that based its worth on spectacle and iconicity over a lived experience. Today we cannot separate this kind of performance from other things. The significant things are those that are "close to us," as Heidegger once said about airplanes and radio sets; the things that are close to us through technology, ultimately, are about the essence of an epoch, but simultaneously also bring us close to one another, physically or through information.[10] For modern architecture, the photographs that captured the buildings in a certain state—that of newness or appearing new—kept the discipline close. But further following this thought, and looking more inward, maintenance is really the thing that brings us close and keeps us close. Its effect of continual newness contributed to a new representation: the photograph.

While the repetition of carefully selected images printed in black and white perpetuated the mythos of modern architecture, the expression of architecture through multiple media and modes of representation is necessary for contemporary projects. Ezra Stoller, the famous photographer whose photographs captured the modern moment, literally rendering the time period, was part of a bygone age; the fixed and singular image is no longer the only thing available, because of the proliferation of media today. These images no longer stand alone, but are instead viewed in the context of other images propped up against other forms of media from videos to blogs, Flickr streams, Instagram feeds, and so on. Architecture that bases its worth on the creation of iconicity and spectacle assumes it will endure in part because it is captured and archived online, instantly and forever available. Recently, the rapid and unprecedented growth primarily in the Middle East and Asia has likewise produced an image culture that is varied yet abundant. While it may be unrealistic to think of limiting a building through a singular or select set of discrete image(s), the way that an image or set of images endures has new meaning in today's endless yet fleeting image culture; this is especially true for buildings that are public and urban.

The recent diversity of architectural works, styles, and ideologies has produced a crisis in the assessment of work and images. Without unifying evaluation criteria across the discipline, we have returned to a focus on performance, examining architecture through the lens of its built life. This is by no means a new concern—we need only remember the American oil crisis of the 1970s, the creation of Paper Architecture, and the beginnings of postmodernism to pull the discipline away from performance into "real architecture." The focus on issues around technology and sustainability is reemerging as a way to think about architecture, but it only exacerbates the split between life and art. This way of thinking is an extension from the late-1990s and early-2000s building boom where realism became subsumed across the disciplines of architecture and art. In many ways architecture during this period leaned heavily on advances in allied fields like structural and climate engineering. Architecture could be advanced only by enveloping other disciplines, and in this moment those particular disciplines were largely based in technology.

Maintenance carries the expression of architecture's essence and represents it as a forward-thinking practice (or not). If maintenance can formulate a line of questioning—in the Heideggerian sense of a "question builds a way" and "the way is one of thinking"[11]—then through maintenance it is possible to see a dialectical relationship with architecture. For instance, the Seattle Public Library, one of the most celebrated buildings of the early twenty-first century, advances the discipline through its form and function, and also through technology. But does it advance beyond its technological bounds? The building is cleaned

0.2
Valérie Kolakis, photograph, *Unbound Steel Wool*, Montreal, Quebec, Canada, 2002. Image courtesy of the artist.

by the most basic and dangerous method: a cleaner on a rope. The use of the squeegee here creates an unmediated relationship between humans and the architecture—bringing the building closer to problems of handicraft. This is a strange way to read a building, with its advanced diagrid façade that collapses structure and enclosure into one system. There is a glamour of the uncelebratory overlaid onto the celebratory, but perhaps there was no other way to solve the problem of cleaning, and the theatrical stunts of the window washer set against the backdrop of the building add to the recursive story of the building, even if it is absurd. We may never know.

Within contemporary architectural discourse, maintenance remains insufficiently defined, except in specialized and technical contexts. Rarely thought of in social or design terms, maintenance has been more readily explored and experimented with in allied disciplines like preservation, material science, development, policy, insurance laws, and building codes. Even as new forms of practice and built work begin to question the limits of its more standard interpretations, the concept of maintenance has not evolved much in recent years.

Furthermore, an important distinction should be made between *cleaning* and *maintenance*. The two are frequently misinterpreted: often maintenance is interpreted as cleaning. But cleaning is more generally associated with domestic, and therefore private and individual, activities: dusting, polishing, or vacuuming. Maintenance instead requires formal organization and teams of skilled workers, operating in public. Where cleaning engages the discrete parts of a building, maintenance is dedicated to safeguarding the holistic image of an architectural work. Each has a unique temporal quality as well. Cleaning is concerned with a building's use at a particular moment; maintenance represents an investment in the persistence of architecture—both as an image and as an ideal.

Maintenance will become increasingly important as architects adopt practices that are to affect environmental performance and also the making of environments.[12] In modernism, architects presented the building cycle with falsely constrained endpoints—conception and realization—that hinged on the parallel production of idealized images.

0.3

Seattle Public Library, window washers
cleaning the façade. Photograph by
Joe Mabel.

These pivotal points have cultivated a narrow understanding of architectural reality, often omitting the life of the building and its performance. An expanded building cycle that incorporates maintenance has the potential to affect the future of architecture by contributing to the cycle of creation, building, occupancy, the representation of architecture, and image circulation, which in turn will impact future invention.

Contemporary artists have pursued the subject of maintenance perhaps more than architects, for whom it is really the most pressing. The artists discussed in this book are often active participants in their work, performing cleaning tasks almost always staged within celebrated works of architecture. Artists choreograph scenes that disrupt iconic images of architecture in order to reveal the tasks of cleaning. In some cases—as with Job Koelewijn's *Cleaning the Rietveld Pavilion* (1992) or Iñigo Manglano-Ovalle's *Le Baiser/The Kiss* (1999)—there is a kind of overperformance for effect, where the artists implement tools and dress associated with a kind of industrial cleaning in excess of both their task and the architecture being cleaned. In so doing they call into question something more than just cleaning. Their works deal with the representation of architecture and with labor that is robust, organized, social, and temporal.

Art practices also reveal technology, and have specifically illuminated the relationship between architecture and the maintenance workers who bring buildings to the forefront of our consciousness through their repetitive labor. Here we can turn to the window washer who exerts forceful energy across a building's face. There is a particular beauty in the striking contrast of the image of the maintenance worker floating in front of a glass curtain wall. The scale of the body against an unrelenting grid has a diminishing effect on the body, but the beauty of the architecture is also disrupted by the image of the worker, reminding one that architecture is not complete. Maintenance in all its clumsy, barebones mechanics is an act of renewal or rebirth, even though it has primarily been thought of as a technical act of repair. In *Morning Cleaning*, for example, Jeff Wall broaches two paradoxical aspects, the everyday and the modern, by staging the event of cleaning. And while the everyday reenacted here is neither flat nor deadpan, it constructs a world that is never revealed.[13]

In architecture culture, maintenance can be understood through two concepts that have been circulating of late: performance and post-occupancy. *Post-occupancy* is a relatively new term that has been adopted into architectural discourse as a means of reconciling the recent and all-too-consuming movement toward realism. Coined to describe the period after a building has been completed, when it has begun to be inhabited, the term places importance on the life of a building rather than on the ideas surrounding its form making. *Post-occupancy* plays off the professional definition of *occupancy*, which describes the number of building users and the building's occupancy type, such as assembly, office, residential, and so on.

Unlike building or design codes, post-occupancy offers calculable elements of knowledge—information or data such as natural elements from temperature to rainfall, or performance-based criteria such as specifications that can be used for evaluation and feedback. It is important to note, however, that these terms should be understood beyond the purely technological—they cannot be separated out from the social or cultural. In a period of tremendous production of the real, it makes sense that there would also be an abundant effort to absorb built work and its effect on discourse. It remains to be seen whether post-occupancy can create a new paradigm for evaluating architecture or effectively support the existing significance attached to form making. Post-occupancy seems to emerge on the side of the owner, the user, the inhabitant, or the specialist, and less so of the design architect, and so there is the danger of it only further fragmenting the discipline. Where post-occupancy takes root is up for grabs; but if it is rethought, it can be a place for new ideas and will deeply affect allied practices in addition to architecture itself.

Interest in preservation and in post-occupancy has come to the forefront over the last two decades, in parallel to the building boom or in spite of it. Most recently, these two subjects were explored through two architecture venues, one an exhibition and the other a book. At the 2010 Venice Biennale, director Kazuyo Sejima of SANAA asked exhibitors to consider the interaction between architecture and its occupants under the title "People meet in architecture." In presenting an entirely new body of work on this topic, the Dutch architect Rem Koolhaas with OMA/AMO curated the exhibition *Cronocaos*, arguing that their work had always been concerned with time and history: "OMA and AMO have been obsessed, from the beginning, with the past."[14] This exhibition presented a select group of materials that became an archive of "fragments" of the total collection of buildings in a range of mediums, from photographs to a series of graphic posters with quotes, charts, and statistics on the subject of preservation; "project cards" made to look like postcards could be torn off a wall and taken with the viewer. The cards featured projects from OMA, including the Maison à Bordeaux, the overscaled fluorescent orange bean bag from the Maison à Bordeaux that was part of another exhibition, *Content*, and oversized photo albums. The posters were used as a place to locate specific quotes on theories about architecture's endurance from critical figures like Ruskin and Viollet-le-Duc. On one exhibition poster, featuring an image of Ruskin and Viollet-le-Duc alongside each other, Ruskin is saying: "Do not let us deceive ourselves in this important matter; it is impossible, as impossible as to raise the dead, to restore anything that has ever been great or beautiful in architecture"; while Viollet-le-Duc declares: "To restore a building is not to repair it, nor to do maintenance, nor to rebuild it, it is to reestablish it in an ultimate state that never existed before." The exhibition announced:

0.4 (following pages)
"Author cleaning reconstructed German Pavilion, Milan Triennale, 1986."
Photograph by Hans Werlemann, courtesy of OMA. Koolhaas's performance is a way of establishing a connection between architecture and its maker.

Introduction

"The interval between the now and the preserved is shrinking, and is about to disappear. From this moment, we do not only have to look back, but also forward; we will have to decide what to preserve in advance."[15] This statement underscores the compression of time between a building's completion and its canonization. To designate a work of architecture a "historic monument" amplifies the burden of care, and raises questions not only around restoration or preservation but also those critical to creative making. Furthermore, deciding "what to preserve in advance" means reclaiming an aspect of the discipline that has been parceled out to specialists and historians. It urges architects to address preservation before a project is realized, and this includes the subject of maintenance, which is new territory in that it has not yet been theorized and the consquences are unknown. And while maintenance may seem like a separate act, not part of the discipline or discourse of architecture, I would argue that there are subtle shifts and slight visual adjustments that are made as a result of maintenance. As buildings go from daily maintenance to larger-scale interventions such as labor done for preservation or restoration, I would still argue that all three things effectively change their appearance. Maintenance performed on a building before it becomes a monument is fundamentally different from when it is performed afterward. Inevitably, there will be codes, practices, and strategies to be put in place when we are trying to uphold a new yet re-created image of the building. If "preservation is overtaking us," maintenance was there first.[16] Preservation is in a way a singular act; maintenance is ongoing. In philosophy, endurance is questioned through a series of acts in looking: for instance, if something passes between an object and a viewer, is it still the same object? If the answer is no, if that object is indeed something other than the original, then this logic could be extended to acts performed on buildings, such as maintenance. In this way, it can be argued that even though the act of maintenance may not leave a trace, it fundamentally changes the image of a building, the image of its architecture. This may not seem particularly significant, but it can open up a new way of thinking whereby architecture is not fixed once a building is complete. Architecture is almost never new and, even more important, its aim should not be to remain new, singular, or fixed. In *Post-Occupancy* (a "special issue" of *Domus*, entrusted to an editor-architect of worldwide renown who illustrates architecture according to his own original codes of communication), Koolhaas presents four projects: the Netherlands Embassy in Berlin, Seattle Central Library, McCormick-Tribune Campus Center at IIT, and Casa da Música. These works, he writes, "represent the realities we were complicit in creating, post-occupancy, as facts, not feats."[17] But these facts are still feats, particularly when they come up against the subject of time.

Maintenance is a reaction to and a momentary covering up of time's terror.[18] Manglano-Ovalle is captured through upclose stills from his film *Le Baiser/The Kiss*, dressed in his orange janitor suit, intently cleaning the glass façade of Mies van der Rohe's Farnsworth House. His pleasure in cleaning is intimately portrayed, perhaps as an attempt to return the house to a place that has been refreshed and reflects the original—"an action for a certain sense of responsibility"—and to avoid "empirical mediocrity."[19]

Maintenance occupies a particular space and moment in the life of a building. It comes after design, after construction drawings—those documents that record the future realities of the project—but exists after building, between acts of building and preservation, and again after preservation or restoration. It would be, in a way, what Jacques Derrida speaks of as "operating in silence, it never leaves any archive of its own."[20] It is only through art that maintenance gets recorded and archived, even if those records are fake, staged fictions. If architecture has had a disciplinary amnesia about maintenance, it was the art world that created "the possibility of memorization of repetition, of reproduction, or of reimpression." And to further this, Derrida goes on to say, "we also must remember that repetition itself, the logic of repetition, indeed the repetition compulsion, remains, according to Freud, indissociable from the death drive. And thus from destruction."[21] Architecture and architects have typically been figures of completion: completing the model, the design, the details, the job site inspection. Maintenance somewhat undoes this completion, requiring us (architects) to be vulnerable and in need of community.[22] If, as Karsten Harries

0.5
Female window washers walking with
ladders. Women working during
World War II. Photograph by David E.
Scheran, 1941. Time & Life Pictures/
Getty Images.

suggests, "What weighs on us is not so much that we are powerless, but that we repress that powerlessness and the associated emotions ... hard to accept our temporality,"[23] and "The historical dimensions of our environment must be preserved and represented if we are to keep open the possibility of genuine dwelling. And we do not preserve or represent history by just playing with its fragments,"[24] I would then argue that sometimes it is only by looking through fragments that a clearer picture of what has occurred can be revealed. Maintenance offers a way of looking at the world, and artists who incorporate maintenance in their work are, in effect, re-presenting architecture back to us.

Each generation draws its own parameters around the discipline: sometimes the role of the architect stops at the idea, sometimes at the drawing, and sometimes at the built work. Each building process requires a unique approach, depending on which aspect the owner, architect, or society prioritizes above all the others: the concept or intent, the construction documents, the physical building, or its reproducible image. It remains to be seen whether architects will choose to stay involved in the constructed lives of their designs, and whether that involvement is even desirable. But one thing that seems to continually be at the core of architecture is its representation.

"Post-occupancy" offers a way to see what happens in the absence of the author; as Koolhaas suggests, maintenance is one component of post-occupancy. Its representation calls into question the very nature of architecture, since the imagery of maintenance, at first blush seeming only technical, would have nothing to do with beauty.[25] The performative aspects of architecture remain repressed; instead, architecture constructs value through idealized representation in publications. Reflecting on architecture in *The Heroic Period of Modern Architecture* (1995), the Smithsons write that the purpose of their book was an exercise in gathering images that meant the most to them personally. This collection, when put together and ordered, made—in their words— a "work-document" that presented photographs and drawings of buildings which constituted a "harmonious whole." The book's mission was to focus on the way modern architecture had been represented through images of completed buildings. The series of black-and-white images collected enabled them to offer a synopsis of the period: "this is probably the last collection of its kind. The next collection in forty years' time of the architecture of our own period will be quite different for it will not record 'buildings,' but built-places, and the documents will be mostly air views, sequential photographs, and system explanations."[26] They conclude (as quoted above): "No one has properly observed a quite definite special sub-category of modern architecture. An architecture of the enjoyment of luxury materials, of the well-made, of the high finish. It is special to Mies and occasional to Le Corbusier and Gropius." In the materials and details of Mies's Barcelona Pavilion, Tugendhat house, and in the Krefeld houses, they find a "shameless bankers' luxuriousness."[27] What in the end, perhaps, the architects realized in their search and curation, and also through their own work, is that there are hidden contingencies yet to be understood by modern architecture. This realization suggests that architectural representation is not just caught up in a particular building, but is indicative of a movement.

While maintenance may initially appear less fundamental to architecture than geometry or other cultural signifiers, it is inextricably tied to the life of buildings. To establish a discourse on maintenance requires us to rethink its associated terms like *cleaning* and *preservation* which, while seemingly banal or misunderstood, have far-reaching implications for the conception, construction, and endurance of buildings and of architecture itself. To use them interchangeably ignores their unique protocols that underscore their social, cultural, environmental, and economic differences. Observations like these aim to affirm the visionary potential of architecture while debunking the imagined reality we attribute to great buildings. An essential aspect of this investigation concerns the labor and efforts necessary to ensure architecture's enduring image. The photographs in this book span the modern and contemporary periods, yet over this long time frame there has been little change in the thinking about endurance, luxury, and the image of architecture with respect to maintenance.

The series of images and short texts included in this book attempt to unpack the history of maintenance in order to understand and uncover its underlying motivations and narratives, as well as alternative models of architecture. The texts are divided into five parts—"Maintenance and the Urban Image," "Cleaning and the Politics of Labor," "Visualizing Decay," "Modernizing Maintenance," and "Post-Occupancy and Alternate Architectural Futures"—with specific buildings, art projects, materials, products, and thematic reflections organized to illustrate each part.

These parts are divided not by type but, rather, by important thematics that run throughout the book. "Maintenance and the Urban Image" deals primarily with the iconography of skyscrapers in the context of the city, in order to set the stage for the relationship between image maintenance and building maintenance that is present throughout. "Cleaning and the Politics of Labor" investigates the differences between public and private maintenance through the lens of those respective workforces. "Visualizing Decay" is the one section exclusively devoted to art practices, illustrating the range of ways artists make issues of maintenance visible. "Modernizing Maintenance" deals with the influx of technology and devices developed to reduce labor, while "Post-Occupancy and Alternate Architectural Futures" looks to a variety of contemporary architectural projects and preservation techniques that deal with the afterlife of buildings in interesting and creative ways. Each part begins with a short paragraph and a project that seems emblematic of the section as a whole. The subsequent short texts address more specific concerns. The result is a collection of small fragments strung together in a larger narrative about how to draw attention to the relationship between architecture and maintenance through an investigation of allied fields.

This book was written as a reflection on the contemporary intersections between architecture, art, and culture. We have just emerged from a period of extensive construction, the building up of cities through important and monumental works of architecture, in some cases undertaken without a totalizing image and in other cases unplanned, even excessive. That is to say: in the rush to build, to make new world(s), there has been little consideration for the unmaking—those things that cause wear and tear on the building, from use to weather, and so on.

19

In the following instances it seems clear that maintenance has been a subject of some interest, but as time passes it will increasingly become an issue for cities in the future, much as it will be for the individual and for society. Maintenance is much more than a metaphor for rethinking culture and society; it exposes a range of imperfections, from unmaking—the decay of buildings, failing joints or chipped glass—to social inequities and unjust labor practices, and to tangible acts that lead to novel design thinking, formal invention, and unprecedented detailing. Even if they are just fragmentary moments, each of these qualities is integral to the underpinning of architecture. This book should be read as a collection of equal images: every image is of equal value. It offers a sort of archive, a curation, a permeable collection that recasts one story about architecture. It is not final; it can be added to or expanded. It is my hope that for someone who reads this book and looks at its images, it will be impossible ever to think about maintenance with indifference, but imperative to recognize that architecture is constructed of several facets, including social facets, one of which is maintenance; and that maintenance can affect design and the creative process.

1

MAINTENANCE AND THE URBAN IMAGE

Architecture relies on a never-ending regime of labor called *maintenance*.[1] The purpose of maintenance is to restore the built environment by offsetting the effects of climate, nature, and time—it is an ongoing, continuous act. Within crowded cities, where maintenance is unavoidably public, it has become a spectacle in its own right through the mirror of reality, fueled by new technologies and novel techniques. This spectacle is especially evident at the site of large, transparent façades where bodies and the distinct machines, apparatuses, materials, performances, and associated techniques of maintenance have become an essential part of the image of the city.

1.1
Window cleaners high up on the
United Nations Building, 1951.
Photograph by Andreas Feininger.
Time & Life Pictures/Getty Images.

Rockefeller Center, Raymond Hood, 1939

Rockefeller Center is the result of a maintenance crisis. Built over the existing Elgin Botanical Garden, which proved too costly to maintain, and with almost no vacant land available in Manhattan, Rockefeller Center emerged as a commercial complex—as an investment and as capital—but it did so by including public space, and by offering cultural and arts-related programs from the Music Hall to the Rainbow Room. In his book *Delirious New York*, Koolhaas writes of the building: "Only the lingering imperfection of the human race casts a shadow in this arena of ecstasy; the architecture is superior to its occupants."[2] In this black-and-white aerial photograph looking down on the window washer, the stark juxtaposition between the occupation of the single man—suspended from the façade by only a belt and hook, cigarette dangling from his mustached mouth—and that of those inside is highlighted.

Koolhaas's collection of images of the Rockettes practicing, getting treatment, and resting presents a stark scene in which these acts take place within windowless spaces, performers in controlled environments for the purpose of commercial effect. The window washer is no different—a singular act on the building façade, like a stage for all to see. But here the tools are primitive, and there is no celebration of "streamlining" or "gracefulness."[3] If Rockefeller Center is exemplary, then, as Koolhaas writes, "the essence and strength of Manhattan is that all its architecture is 'by committee' and that committee is Manhattan's inhabitants themselves."[4] Including the window washer, who has been left out of the story.

1.2

A New York window washer strapped to the side of the RCA Building in Rockefeller Center, with St. Patrick's Cathedral below him to the left, 1961. Photograph by William Lovelace © FLC/ARS.

Façade of Pharos Building, Vanessa van Dam, 2002

In 2002 the Dutch artist Vanessa van Dam created a window-washing installation for the Pharos Building outside Amsterdam, designed by Kohn Pedersen Fox. She had been commissioned by the Rijksgebouw-endienst Institute to design a welcoming gesture for the façade, given the building's proximity to the Schiphol Airport train line. Although it never came to fruition, the proposal calls attention to architecture's relationship with maintenance and, more importantly, to the image of this relationship.[5] Van Dam proposed to install eighty-five industrial-sized window wipers on the building's glass façade that would respond individually to a programmed script activated by sensors in tune with the local weather conditions. With Amsterdam's frequent rain, they would often be in action, either synchronized or waving at their own rate. Van Dam recollects: "I thought it would be very 'poetic' that you would be greeted literally by eighty-five waving 'arms.'"[6]

In lieu of a physical installation, the project has endured in the form of a (strikingly realistic) rendered photo-collage. The image of the mechanized façade in action, ever vigilant against the effects of weather and dirt, embodies the modernist injunction of cleanliness; the heavy black arms contrasting with the transparent glass and aluminum façade bring maintenance to the foreground of our attention. Here cleanliness is an object of mechanized fantasy that threatens to overtake the architecture itself. The over-scaled wipers in the Photoshop rendering for van Dam's proposal are reminiscent of images that show the window-washing gondola at Lever House decades earlier, or more recent robotic inventions like PIRO's Windoro bot or GEKKO's solar-panel-cleaning robot.[7]

Bernard Khoury's Bank of Beirut Headquarters (2004) bears striking similarities to van Dam's proposal. Khoury uses windshield wipers from cars to clean the bank's glass curtain wall, creating a pattern of clean quarter-circles in the dust of the façade they cannot reach. In this case, however, the wipers are also suggestive of the building's relationship to financial and institutional cleanliness and transparency— or lack thereof.

For both Khoury and van Dam, it is clearly the image of window washing to which they want to call our attention. Neither wiper mechanism is particularly efficient at cleaning, but they remind us that the labor of building maintenance—unlike with cars or with airplanes—is not accepted as being "close to us."[8]

1.3
Vanessa van Dam, *Façade of Pharos
Building*, 2002. Courtesy of the artist.

Maintenance and the Urban Image

Capturing Cleanliness

In the late nineteenth century, window washers attracted much public interest. They began as a fixture on the street, with their transportable ladders and their cleaning devices, and by the turn of the century they had moved up to the high floors of skyscrapers.

Working up in the air was a novel byproduct of the Industrial Era, as growing institutions and corporations required physical expansion. Indeed, the profession was remarked upon in a July 1937 *Popular Science* article about a nationwide radio broadcast by two window washers, one in Chicago and one in New York, from the outside of buildings they were cleaning.[9] Offices, factories, and corporate headquarters quickly became essential building types, but their size and complexity demanded far more maintenance labor and technology than buildings in the past. This work required a particular set of skills and expertise, as well as new sorts of equipment.[10] The economic growth and prosperity that made such large buildings possible also created a new economic class. Property owners were financially distinct from the men who serviced their buildings, and the organized action of workers moving up and down the façade sustained the visibility of this disparity.

Initially, window washers who worked on the exterior of window frames and walls at buildings like the Empire State Building and Rockefeller Center had to climb through the windows, clip themselves onto the exterior, wash the window with a hand-held squeegee, and then climb back inside after the window was finished (see figure 1.4). This was a tedious job—and one of the riskiest at the time—requiring workers to move continuously between inside and outside while balancing on a thin ledge. In this scenario, the window washer would have to interact with the office workers as he went inside and out, disrupting their tasks.

By the mid-twentieth century, the limits and boundaries of the workspace were somewhat redefined by new buildings like Lever House and other corporate headquarters, but social divisions were still clearly demarcated. Above the street, the maintenance worker was both removed from the general public and alienated from those working inside the building. Especially with the development of curtain-wall systems, which often had inoperable windows, the inside clearly belonged to one economic class while the outside belonged to another. The façade became a line of separation—not only a physical boundary separating inside from out, but also a division between two classes of workers, each visibly exposed to the other and each on display.

Modernism sought to minimize this spectacle of maintenance through technology. The idea was to create a fixed building image that could be maintained by devices like the squeegee, tilt windows, and window-washing rigs rather than by people. Buildings had to be kept in order to preserve their relationship to the photographs of them distributed in books and magazines, to always retain their immediate post-construction imageability. Such an ambition could be achieved only through limiting dependence on a profusion of technological devices and gadgets to keep the building looking as intended.

1.4 (following pages)
Precarious work: A window washer using a leather safety harness as he works on the exterior of the Empire State Building, New York, circa 1935. Photograph by Al Gretz/Keystone View Company/FPG/Archive Photos/Getty Images.

33

1.5
Lever House as shown in Reyner
Banham's *The Architecture of the
Well-Tempered Environment*, 1969.

Lever House, SOM, 1952

The close-up, black-and-white photograph of the Lever Brothers' company headquarters that appears in architecture critic and historian Reyner Banham's book *The Architecture of the Well-Tempered Environment* features the tower's ultra-smooth curtain wall and an empty window-washing rig, hovering just above the façade.[11] In the accompanying text, Banham describes the novel technical details that enable the thinness of the curtain wall, but he makes no mention of the window-washing gondola. While this was not the first window-washing rig to exist, Lever House did have the first large-scale façade designed specifically to accommodate a motorized gondola, with stainless steel mullions and tracks built into the façade.[12]

The emerging office of Skidmore, Owings and Merrill (SOM) designed the Midtown Manhattan headquarters to emphasize the façade and its sleek glass curtain wall. The building's configuration consists of a tower above an elevated base and open public courtyard. With its main elevation set back from the street and perpendicular to Park Avenue, the tower orients the bulk of its surface area toward traffic, operating as a large billboard.

The orientation of the façade meant that the full-time window washing became a kind of promotional act. It served as an advertisement for a pristine and modern lifestyle and also for the Lever Brothers company, which had a long history of producing soap and other domestic cleaning products. It is at once a recursive act of architecture and a reflection of the emerging society of 1950s America, so that maintenance is integral to the design of the Lever House façade. Through the glass curtain wall's repeated cleaning and renewal efforts, maintenance no longer acts as a sign; it becomes a signifier without a signified, an advertisement without a product.

The façade requires an industrial kind of upkeep that is foreign to its internal maintenance. This separation allows a building's maintenance workers to formulate strategies specific to interior versus exterior. The exterior of a building develops very particular maintenance demands, delineating conditions associated with vision. Exterior maintenance

has become identified with the form of the outside of the building, rather than its internal functions. Aside from the fact that continuous curtain walls and inoperable windows make exterior cleaning necessary, the surface area of large buildings like Lever House is too great to be adequately managed by an interior cleaning staff. Maintenance of the curtain wall is therefore a function that follows form.

The typical American office building is maintained by a workforce that is separate from the office's employees, as opposed to housekeeping, which is typically done in close proximity to the owner or by the owner him- or herself. Window washing lacks the intimacy of housecleaning, but the window washer occupies an important space between the building and its exterior—between the building's internal life and the city beyond. The maintenance worker is intimate with the life inside the high-rise while moving up and down the face of the building, yet he or she is also fundamentally separate from that interior life.

It is important to note that the interior life of buildings constructed in the early 1950s increasingly began to include women. In Lever House as well as other major American corporate headquarters, these women occupied desks exposed to the exterior, where they would come face to face with the window washer, reversing the spectacle of domesticity. The theoretical discourse of the 1990s spent a considerable amount of time on surveillance and the voyeur, but most of this discourse was concerned exclusively with the domestic; historians and critics focused primarily on the housewife, on her position within the home and in society, but they spent little time on the relationship between the public and the maintenance worker.

When we reconsider buildings like Lever House, however, it is clear that there is a loaded dynamic between its maintenance, use, and function as urban spectacle. The same is certainly true for other midcentury skyscrapers, and for so many buildings today. It is time for the role of maintenance in the urban environment to be rethought.

1.6–1.7
Skidmore, Owings and Merrill,
Lever House, New York, 1952.
Image courtesy of SOM.

Maintenance and the Urban Image

1.8
Jennifer Bolande, *Landmark Acquisition #1*,
1998–1999, 22 × 13½ in., pencil and
gouache on newsprint. Image courtesy
of the artist.

Appliance House, Jennifer Bolande, 1998–1999

In her project *Appliance House* (1998–1999), artist Jennifer Bolande examines Lever House as a technical and mechanical object. Bolande critiques Lever House's status as a modern icon through techniques of drawing, collage, and photography. Drawing over a newspaper advertisement from the *New York Times*, she creates a new series of advertisements based on the building's sale. In one example, the insertion of pencil marks in a gridded pattern of rectangles over the words *Landmark Acquisition* creates a level of informality at odds with the precision of the building's design—the pencil marks emphasize the human hand over mechanized construction.

This light touch upon the building's elevation is similar to the touch of the window washer's hand on the glass façade. Art critic Katy Siegel writes: "Bolande rhymes the two kinds of relics, the two kinds of cubes, the upper and lower parts of Manhattan's East Side, and the opposite ends of the laundry-soap biz."[13] Bolande's work helps set Lever House apart from its Park Avenue neighbors, renewing the social and cultural power latent in the building.

Influenced by a series of photographs taken of an appliance store, where the appliances are illuminated through fluorescent ceiling lights typically found in showroom-like spaces, she transfers them into a collage of negatives stacked upon each other to form the profile of Lever House. Bolande similarly references technology, image, and cleaning in an earlier work entitled *Windshield* (1989) that is almost a façade mock-up or prototype for a new curtain-wall system; here she carefully cleans away a space on the glass in the pattern of a window wiper, but the blade is absent. This fascination with the mechanical device for cleaning is shared by van Dam's proposed installation for the Pharos building, where over-scaled wipers and gaskets are out of proportion with familiar, more delicate automotive windshield wiper blades. In the case of a high-rise tower, the scale of the airplane wiper is closer to the tower than that of a car wiper. The size of the wiper reveals something about the design of the curtain wall—that it is not fine, but has thickness, depth, and requires intensive labor to keep it looking new.

KODAK SAFETY FILM 5079
21 21A 22 22A 23 23A 24 24A
5079
KODAK SAFETY FILM 5079
KODAK SAFETY FILM 5079
26 26A 27 27A 28 28A 29 29A
KODAK SAFETY FILM 5079
31 31A 32 32A 33 33A 34 34A
KODAK SAFETY FILM 5079
1 1A 2 2A 3 3A 4 4A
5079
KODAK SAFETY FILM 5079
6 6A 7 7A 8 8A 9 9A 10
KODAK SAFETY FILM 5079
11 11A 12 12A 13 13A 14 14A
5079
KODAK SAFETY FILM 5079

1.9
Jennifer Bolande, *Detail of Appliance House*, 1998–1999, Duratrans photo in stainless steel lightboxes. Image courtesy of the artist.

1.10
Jennifer Bolande, *Windshield*, 1989, 33 × 66 × 13 in., chalk on chalkboard, glass, rubber, wood, aluminum. Photograph by E. P. Wilson. Image courtesy of the artist.

1.11
Jennifer Bolande, *Cast of Characters*,
1999, 18 × 23 in., Type C print.
Courtesy of the artist.

In *Cast of Characters*, Bolande superimposes photographs of model refrigerators and washers along with appliance-sized cardboard boxes and images of Mies van der Rohe's Lake Shore Drive Apartments. It is well known that Mies had to rework the interior layout of the units dozens of times until finally settling on a more normative arrangement, with the living room located in the corner. The collage of the two residential towers repeated as an arrangement of four is something that Mies was never able to achieve in reality. 900–910 Lake Shore Drive would be built later, but not in the same way or with the same details, due to 860–880's experimental structural system and building sway that caused a failure in the windows and rain leakage. The actual point of failure was the operable upper sash of the window wall, designed to rotate so that the tenant could clean the glass.[14] Over time, however, the effects of gravity on its structural system—steel frame encased in concrete to make it fireproof—would add too much weight to the frame, causing the window wall to deflect and producing gaps around the windows. After the structural frame was built and encased in concrete, to comply with city building codes, the visible I-beam steel girders that give the building its complete and unified appearance were added. The transparency of Lake Shore Drive is achieved through this steel structure, the first of all such tall structures. Even the bedrooms were transparent. What was important was to have a visual order at the perimeter and a consistent light-gray curtain at the surface closest to the glass, with a second interior layer hung from an inner track, to be chosen by the tenant.

Bolande's layering of appliances on top of the façades reveals the real problem at Lake Shore Drive: tenants inserted individual box air conditioners, as the building was built without air-conditioning. At 900–910, air-conditioning was installed: the first of its kind in an apartment building in Chicago. Here the façade would also shift toward a unitized system and large-scale allover use of tinted glass.[15]

43

La Notte, Michelangelo Antonioni, 1961

The opening sequence of director Michelangelo Antonioni's film *La Notte* (1961) is comprised of two slow, continuous pans of architect Gio Ponti's Pirelli Tower in Milan. The first pan presents a scene unfolding from the street, then the camera shifts from the ground up to the top of the tower. In the next sequence, the camera moves to the uppermost floor and slowly pans out across the roof underneath a slight canopy at the very top of the building, showing the rail of the window rig. As the camera approaches the edge of the building, a panorama of the city is revealed. (The Pirelli Tower was the tallest building in Italy at the time *La Notte* was filmed.) The camera descends the façade as though from the perspective of a window washer working on a rig, shifting the view inward, from city to building. As the camera shifts downward during the nearly two-and-a-half-minute introduction, the transparency of the façade shifts with the changing light, from day to night, and down along its entire length. The film makes available a privileged view of Milan's skyline from the unfamiliar perspective of the window washer. The all-glass façade reflects the city and extends its panorama. As the camera descends, the view turns toward the building, mixing the reflection of the city in the glass with the transparency that reveals the Tower's inner life. This is a rare instance where the viewer sees what the maintenance worker sees.

1.12–1.14
Film stills, *La Notte*, 1961.

Maintenance and the Urban Image

1.15

Skidmore, Owings and Merrill, Sears Tower, Chicago, 1974. The color photograph offers an awe-inspiring image of man and machine literally together at the top of one of the world's largest and most iconic towers. The engineer inspects the window-washing machine. Image courtesy of SOM.

Sears Tower, SOM, 1973

We stand at the beginning, not the end, of a culture-period.
We await entirely new miracles of technology and chemistry.
Let us never forget it.
Reyner Banham, "The Glass Paradise"[16]

The Sears Tower—now known as Willis Tower—served as the corporate headquarters for Sears, Roebuck & Co. when it was completed in 1973. At the time it was the tallest building in the world, designed to accommodate all of Sears's 350,000 employees, with room for future growth. The building, known for its structural ingenuity, is a series of nine towers bundled together at various heights to allow light in and meet setback requirements.

Images of the Sears Tower capture acts of urban maintenance that reveal the simultaneous trajectories of maximized mechanical technology and ad hoc, low-wage human capital. At the time of its construction it was at the forefront of optimum, real-time upkeep. The façade is made of black, anodized aluminum panels with 16,100 bronze-tinted glass windows. It relies on six roof-mounted robots, all operated remotely by an engineer, to roam and clean its enormous surface eight times a year. The curtain wall includes built-in tracks to accommodate their vertical movement.

Building on earlier precedents, the Sears Tower eliminates the need for laborers working in dangerous conditions, while projecting the image of a technological utopia. The images contradict our traditional notions of effortless architectural permanence.

Chapter 1

Corporate Materiality and Self-Maintenance:
Alcoa, U.S. Steel, and PPG

No epoch advanced the concept of being "maintenance-free" more than the 1950s to 1980s in America, a period defined by a series of important innovations in the building industry that were quickly integrated into daily life by increasingly large-scale corporations.

Between 1953 and 1984, three major corporations began to dramat- ically influence the American built landscape. The Aluminum Company of America (Alcoa), U.S. Steel, and Pittsburgh Plate Glass (PPG) all symbolized American ingenuity in construction. As these three industries evolved in the mid-twentieth century, the idea of iconic corporate headquarters came into being.

In early models it was a high priority, as with Lever House, that headquarters communicate an image of cleanliness to the public. Following suit, the Pittsburgh three—Alcoa, U.S. Steel, and PPG—each built offices that used architecture to reflect the mission of the company, constructing their buildings with the materials they produced: aluminum, steel, and glass respectively.[17] Each added to the Pittsburgh skyline and exerted their corporate identity over the city with the latest and most significant material advancements.

Building materials underwent radical developments in the 1970s, as corporations experimented with nanotechnologies and material science. Emerging from this building boom was the idea that if the materials were durable, the building's image (and therefore the company's) would endure as well. It became important to each of these three companies that the architecture of their headquarters should reflect the most progressive examples of their products.

1.16
Phillip Johnson and John Burgee,
One PPG Place, Pittsburgh, 1984.

The Alcoa Building (1953), designed by Wallace Harrison and Max Abramovitz, was the first aluminum skyscraper, impressive for its economic and lightweight curtain-wall system. The stamped, floor-to-ceiling façade panels are only one-eighth inch thick, and the heating and cooling system is tucked under the floors to save space.[18] Not to be outmatched, the U.S. Steel Building—also designed by Harrison and Abramovitz—remains the tallest building in Pittsburgh since it was completed in 1971. The U.S. Steel tower is widely considered innovative for its exposed Cor-ten steel girders (a new material at the time) that were filled with liquid to prevent fire.[19] By 1984, further advancements in curtain-wall design allowed Philip Johnson and John Burgee to use close to a million square feet of Solarban PPG-brand glass in the façade of PPG Place.[20]

The emergence of these American corporations offers an extraordinary opportunity to examine the historical intersection of maintenance, architecture, and materiality. The ability of products or materials to speak to a kind of "national virtue" in America, beyond the idea of cleanliness, was of great importance in the conception of the headquarters themselves.

Another important shift during this epoch was the transition from modernism to postmodernism, and changing attitudes toward architectural aesthetics. Buildings no longer needed to be so white and pure, but as architecture historian and critic Mark Wigley points out in his book *White Walls, Designer Dresses*, "As always, everything is a question of surface."[21] Even if whiteness and transparency ceased to be important architectural paradigms, the ability to maintain the image of each of these three prominently sited headquarters buildings was paramount. The buildings needed to be able to self-clean.

1.17

Harrison, Abramovitz & Abbe Architects, architectural model, U.S. Steel Building, Pittsburgh, 1971. Image courtesy of the Abramovitz Archive, Avery Architectural and Fine Arts Library, Columbia University.

The PPG headquarters, for instance, is made of highly reflective black glass. The reflectivity of the glass broadcasts the image of Pittsburgh back to the surrounding buildings, while the dark color helps to minimize the appearance of dirt. The U.S. Steel Building takes a different approach, as it is constructed primarily of Cor-ten steel, designed to weather the elements with little need for maintenance—the metal oxidizes and forms a brown coating that protects the material from further corrosion, minimizing the need for significant external maintenance.

Built several decades earlier than PPG or U.S. Steel, the Alcoa Building did not exactly self-clean, but it did incorporate a certain degree of maintenance forethought into the design of the façade. Given the danger and complexity of hanging off the exterior to clean windows, Alcoa's aluminum windows were specifically designed to pivot so that they could be cleaned from the inside.[22] All three buildings sought to reduce the need for maintenance workers on their surface, prioritizing their function as stable iconic images.

In this way, corporate headquarters became an important site of experimental architecture—a testing ground for material innovations. Corporations went to great lengths to distinguish themselves with their buildings, to set themselves apart from other companies that had already staked their claim in American cities.

Union Carbide Headquarters, Natalie de Blois/SOM, 1962

Architect, teacher, and activist Natalie de Blois spent thirty years of her half-century career working in the New York City (1944–1962) and Chicago (1962–1974) offices of SOM. She was first a designer in the New York City office, helping to define the forms of midcentury corporate modernism, particularly the glass-and-steel office tower typology that housed complex international organizations. These corporations and the large architectural firms that designed their headquarters adopted the organizational structures they served, reshaping the nature of professional practice. Yet, even as a key author of the architectural language of international corporate modernism, de Blois has largely been excluded from histories of the period, overshadowed by her renowned colleague, architect and SOM partner Gordon Bunshaft.

De Blois's career reflects the difficulties faced by a female American professional in the mid-twentieth century, and while she was not the only woman at SOM, the intricacies of her struggle as an architect are unprecedented. Despite holding a leadership position within the office, she was never rewarded with partner status. Tracing her career reveals a multitude of challenges faced by architects of both genders during this time, and highlights SOM's rapid transformation into one of the largest architecture offices in the world—one that framed itself as a design firm offering more than technical expertise.

53

1.18 (following pages)
Harrison, Abramovitz & Abbe Architects, U.S. Steel Building; note Cor-Ten steel curtain wall detail drawing (1952). Image courtesy of the Abramovitz Archive, Avery Architectural and Fine Arts Library, Columbia University.

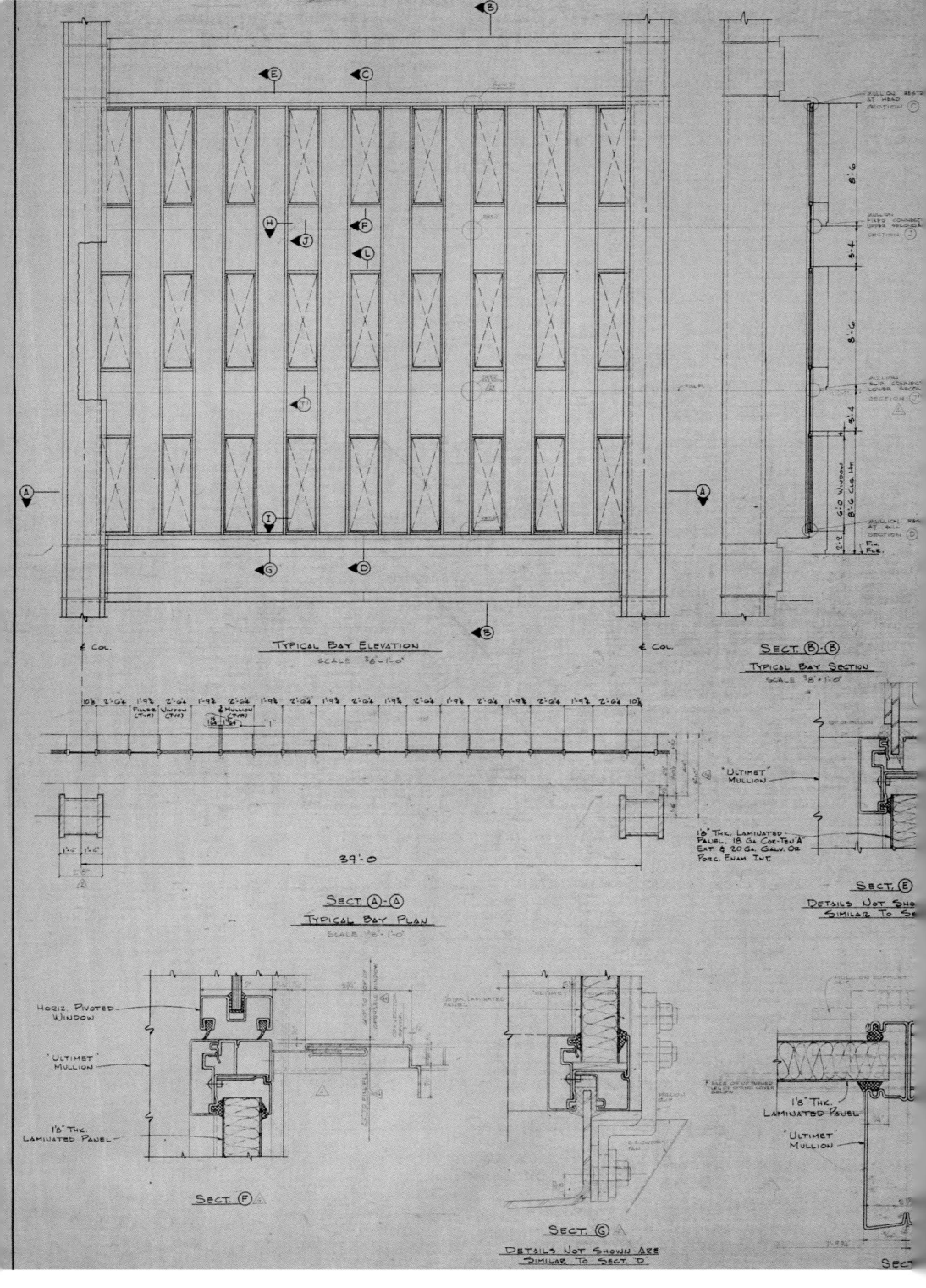

TYPICAL BAY ELEVATION
SCALE ⅜"=1'-0"

SECT. A-A
TYPICAL BAY PLAN
SCALE ⅜"=1'-0"

SECT. B-B
TYPICAL BAY SECTION
SCALE ⅜"=1'-0"

"ULTIMET" MULLION

1⅛" THK. LAMINATED PANEL, 18 GA. COR-TEN "A" EXT. & 20 GA. GALV. OR PORC. ENAM. INT.

SECT. E
DETAILS NOT SHO
SIMILAR TO SE

HORIZ. PIVOTED WINDOW

"ULTIMET" MULLION

1⅛" THK. LAMINATED PANEL

SECT. F

SECT. G
DETAILS NOT SHOWN ARE
SIMILAR TO SECT. D.

1⅛" THK. LAMINATED PANEL

"ULTIMET" MULLION

SECT

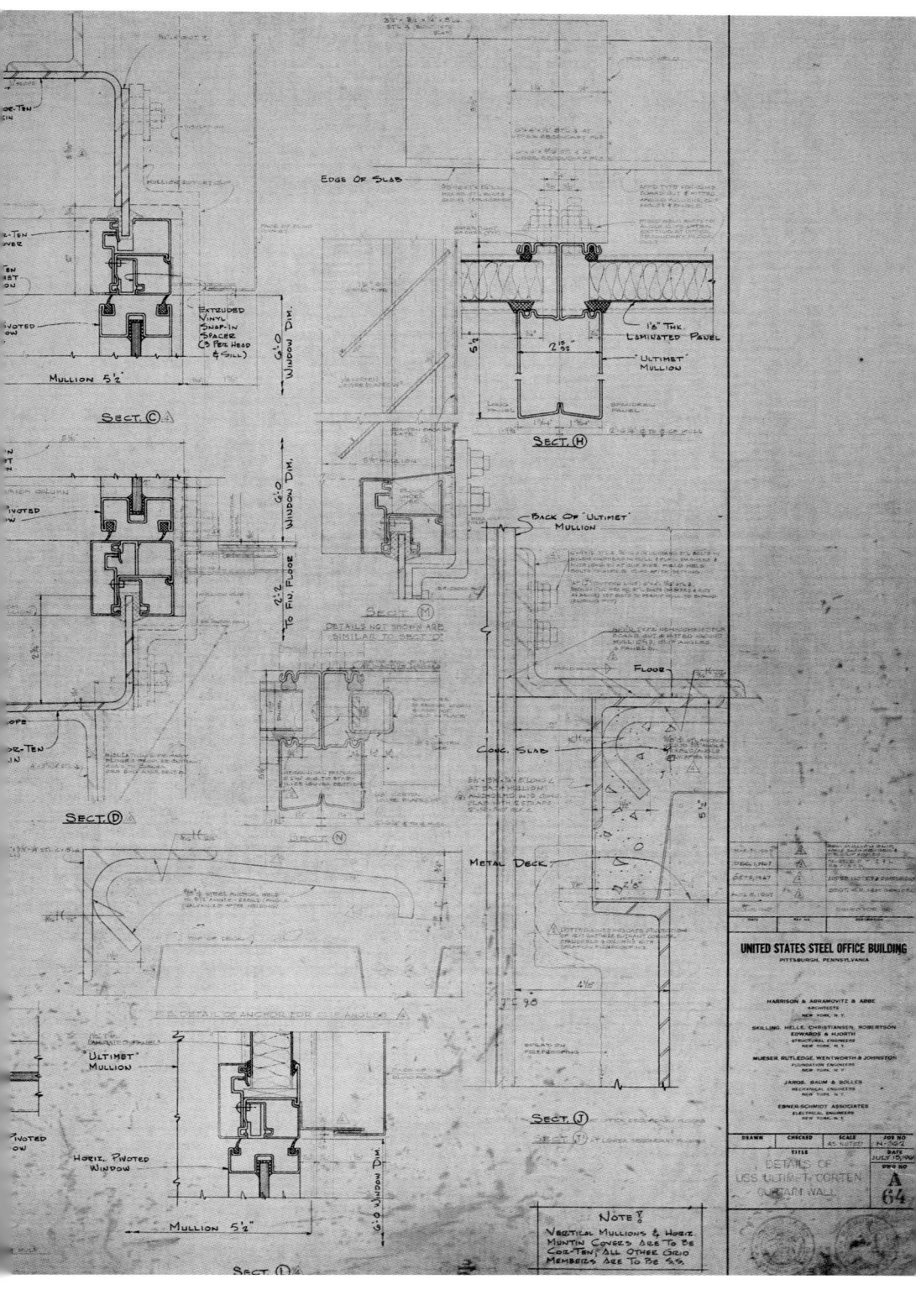

MULLION 5½"

SECT. C

EXTRUDED
VINYL
SNAP-IN
SPACER
(3 PER HEAD
& SILL)

EDGE OF SLAB

⅛" THK. LAMINATED PANEL

"ULTIMET" MULLION

2⁵⁄₃₂"

SECT. H

SECT. D

SECT. M

DETAILS NOT SHOWN ARE
SIMILAR TO SECT. "D"

SECT. N

BACK OF "ULTIMET" MULLION

FLOOR

CONC. SLAB

METAL DECK

SECT. J

P.B. DETAIL OF ANCHOR FOR CLIP ANGLES

"ULTIMET" MULLION

HORIZ. PIVOTED WINDOW

MULLION 5½"

SECT. L

NOTE:
VERTICAL MULLIONS & HORIZ.
MUNTIN COVERS ARE TO BE
COR-TEN; ALL OTHER GRID
MEMBERS ARE TO BE S.S.

UNITED STATES STEEL OFFICE BUILDING
PITTSBURGH, PENNSYLVANIA

HARRISON & ABRAMOVITZ & ABBE
ARCHITECTS
NEW YORK, N.Y.

SKILLING, HELLE, CHRISTIANSEN, ROBERTSON
EDWARDS & HJORTH
STRUCTURAL ENGINEERS
NEW YORK, N.Y.

MUESER, RUTLEDGE, WENTWORTH & JOHNSTON
FOUNDATION ENGINEERS
NEW YORK, N.Y.

JAROS, BAUM & BOLLES
MECHANICAL ENGINEERS
NEW YORK, N.Y.

EBNER-SCHMIDT ASSOCIATES
ELECTRICAL ENGINEERS
NEW YORK, N.Y.

| DRAWN | CHECKED | SCALE | JOB NO |
| | | AS NOTED | 14-762 |

TITLE
DETAILS OF
USS ULTIMET CORTEN
CURTAIN WALL

DATE
JULY 15, 1964

DWG NO
A 64

1.19

Harrison, Abramovitz & Abbe Architects,
U.S. Steel Building, aerial photograph
(1952). Image courtesy of the Abramovitz
Archive, Avery Architectural and Fine Arts
Library, Columbia University.

By 1948, de Blois was working alongside Bunshaft on many seminal projects—including Lever House (1952), Hilton Istanbul (1955), and the Connecticut General Life Insurance Company Headquarters (1956)—and later as the senior designer on the Union Carbide Corporation Headquarters (1960) and Pepsi-Cola Corporation World Headquarters (1960). Three of these projects—Lever House, Union Carbide, and Pepsi-Cola—are sited along Park Avenue in New York City. She was a professionally marginalized figure who primarily provided visions for worlds in which women were more generally marginalized.[23] De Blois designed the modern American workplace, where women, who largely played supportive roles, were visible in open-plan configurations but invisible within the corporations' higher ranks. Nowhere is this more apparent than in the Lever and Union Carbide headquarters. Behind the taut, glazed curtain walls, predominantly female administrative assistants sat within the open floor plan, while male managers occupied private offices with city views. Corporations around the globe adopted these towers, replicating both the internal organizational structure of the American corporation and its physical form, appearance, and gender politics.

While de Blois strove to implement new ways of working that aimed to increase productivity and flow, she also designed social environments. It is now possible to reflect on the way these spaces restricted advancement, mirroring de Blois's inability to break through the "glass ceiling." It was through these projects, and others that de Blois led between 1952 and 1960, that she became intimately familiar with the challenges of headquarters design as well as the corporate politics of the clients she served—politics much like those she experienced at SOM. The 1955 SOM newsletter featured scenes of the New York office with de Blois at her drafting desk, the only woman in the image. This, however, seemed to bother her little when she spoke with Betty Blum in 2004:

"Well, do you think that you were treated fairly?"

"Was I treated? Oh, yes, for what I am, I was treated fairly. Sure." She continues: "Being a woman architect is not the important thing to me. I've always been singled out because I'm the one who did large buildings, but architecture is a building profession."

Union Carbide, among all of the buildings at this time, would become the most integrated into the city, submerging its structure below ground to negotiate the subway and investing in a new image of the skyline along Park Avenue. Taller and more complex than almost any previous SOM building, Union Carbide has an incredibly hierarchical interior office plan, and would be among these new buildings that required a "plan of action" for managing both interior and exterior cleaning.[24]

1.20
Alcoa Building, 2007, digital photograph.
Image courtesy of Meredith Clausen.

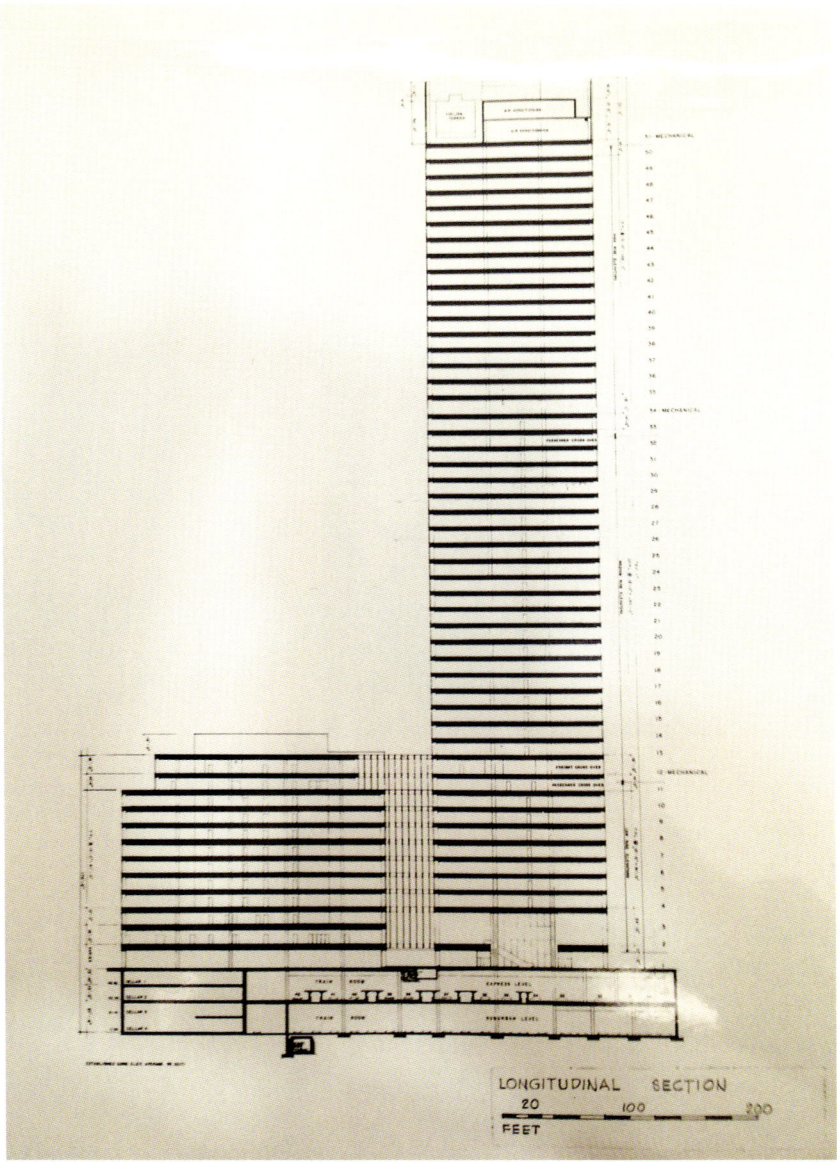

1.21
Skidmore, Owings and Merrill,
Union Carbide Building, section.
Image courtesy of SOM.

Maintenance and the Urban Image

1.22

Alfred Wolf, *Pyramid, Alpine Cleaners.* Cleaning
I. M. Pei's pyramid at the Louvre Museum.
In order to clean the Pyramid, mountain climbers
were trained to clean windows (as opposed
to the apparently more difficult task of teaching
window washers to climb mountains).

The Louvre Pyramid, Pei Cobb Freed & Partners, 1989

The Pyramid at the Louvre had a Bilbao effect before Bilbao. The Pyramid, in its rareness of form, is at once highly referential to ancient structures and structurally innovative. It gave the historic and world-famous Louvre Museum an iconic and contemporary image, and as a result almost ten million visitors pass through the Pyramid's new entrance to the Louvre every year.

In 2009, the Louvre celebrated the twentieth anniversary of the opening of the all-glass Pyramid designed by I. M. Pei. As part of the celebration, the museum showcased its "alpinists"—mountain climbers trained as window washers—washing its glass walls.

At its original opening, critics referred to the Pyramid as "a gigantic gadget."[25] It was initially controversial for its shape and material, but even more controversy ensued over how to maintain its sloping glass walls. The solution was to hire mountain climbers to clean, as opposed to teaching window washers to climb. For a brief moment, these climber-washers were replaced with a mechanized, robotic cleaning device and, in effect, "the gigantic gadget" was being cared for by another gadget.

The absence of people cleaning the façade lends the Pyramid a certain appearance of permanence. Without the visibility of human labor and upkeep, the building seems to be self-sufficient. In their work and their presence, janitors and window washers are measures of time; as time passes, façades get dirty. The window washers' work is specific to the surface of the building. The removal of the person and his or her replacement with a mechanized device reframes the building and changes our perception of it.

W.P. FRITH. R.A. PINX^T   C.W. SHARPE. SCULP^T

THE CROSSING SWEEPER.

FROM THE PICTURE IN THE COLLECTION OF W. HOULDSWORTH, ESQ: HALIFAX.

LONDON. JAMES S. VIRTUE

2

CLEANING AND THE POLITICS OF LABOR

Industrialization brought about great shifts in the maintenance of the city and the upkeep of the home in the late nineteenth century. Cities that in earlier years had no institutionalized methods of public sanitation began to develop officially recognized, organized labor forces to clean them. Whole new professions and techniques were developed to facilitate this process—from the street sweeper to the window washer high up on the newly emerging skyscrapers. At the same time, advances in environmental and structural technologies as well as new material developments allowed modern architects to envision a new way of life, a sanitized domestic environment full of light and space while free of clutter and excess. However, their white walls and extensive glass curtain walls also established new hierarchies between the inhabitants of modern buildings and the people who maintained them, fomenting certain social conditions that had not necessarily existed before.

"Manifesto for Maintenance Art," Mierle Laderman Ukeles, 1969

Mierle Laderman Ukeles takes the purpose of housework to task in her 1969 "Manifesto for Maintenance Art," applying typical forms of domestic work to the maintenance of the art museum. Without attempting to transform maintenance tasks themselves, she draws important connections between two fields that had long been dissociated:

> Now, I will simply do these maintenance everyday things, and flush them up to consciousness, exhibit them, as Art. I will live in the museum as I customarily do at home with my husband and my baby, for the duration of the exhibition. ... I will sweep and wax the floors, dust everything, wash the walls ... cook, [and] invite people to eat.

Ukeles sets up her proposal through the opposition of two basic systems:

> The Death Instinct: separation; individuality; Avant-Garde par excellence; to follow one's own path to death—do your own thing; dynamic change. ...
>
> The Life Instinct: unification; the eternal return; the perpetuation and maintenance of the species' survival systems and operations; equilibrium. ...
>
> Development: pure individual creation; the new; change; progress; advance; excitement; flight or fleeing. ...
>
> Maintenance: keep the dust off the pure individual creation; preserve the new; sustain the change; protect progress; defend and prolong the advance; renew the excitement; repeat the flight.[1]

2.2
Mierle Laderman Ukeles, *Hartford Wash: Washing, Tracks, Maintenance: Outside*, 1973. Image courtesy of Ronald Feldman Fine Arts, New York.

The two systems, development and maintenance, are identified with two instincts, death and life, respectively. It is immediately clear that Ukeles is borrowing her terminology from Sigmund Freud, and initially it seems contradictory to link the death instinct with development, as the latter is usually thought to be creative, not destructive.[2] The death drive, or Thanatos, withdraws into itself toward unbinding energy. Also called the ego instinct, this drive is self-preserving, sometimes cruelly so, and will refuse to bind with anything that threatens the ego (an apt description of many architects).

We can draw parallels between the ego instinct and the heroic quality of early avant-garde modernism and its following generation. This type of work is glorified in our society, which values linear development and invention over endurance. The death drive manifests itself as aggression toward the object world, for the developer is constantly driven to replace the existing model with a new one. This drive requires complete expenditure of resources, as all energy and effort are applied toward new ideas—ideas that will separate the developer from those who came before. In its attempt to stay contemporary, modernism had to continually flee from the past in order to assert the new.

On the other hand, the life or sexual drive looks toward binding its energy with others—seeking "unification," as Ukeles puts it—and hopes to perpetuate something that is already present, to renew. Sustaining, protecting, defending, and repeating are all ways of maintaining as they all seek to connect, to renew, and to sustain desire. For Ukeles, the binding nature of the life drive was not an abstract concept: she experienced it on a daily basis. "When I had a baby, I realized that my language needed to open up out of the 'I.' O.K., I'm changing my baby's diaper. The baby's crying. The baby needs, the baby; the baby needs. The need is not in me, it's outside in another human being. ... I fell madly in love with this child. So I became a maintenance worker."[3]

Ukeles's claim that the life drive of maintenance sustains change, however, seems contradictory. Maintenance involves returning a creation to a prior condition, but sustaining change is more than making something like new; it is fostering development by replenishing the resources that development necessarily consumes. As Ukeles explains further: "I had never worked so hard in my life as when I had a little baby ... I was working like a maniac. But there were no words in the culture that gave value for the work I was doing."[4] She points to the disconnect between housework and, ultimately, maintenance and art. As an artist, she distinctly feels how the two are at odds in our culture: "I felt like I was two completely different people. ... I no longer knew who I was. I got so pissed off."[5]

While Ukeles's manifesto focused on the relationship between private maintenance tasks and public art, her proposal for the exhibit *Care* would have turned the museum into her home, not only making the public institution a private place but also turning the private into a public event. This process would have included making other stories about maintenance and sustenance public. Ukeles proposed to make people aware of the environmental consequences of waste through the abuse of resources like water, air, and land. She later said: "It was such fantasy, right? But I actually believed that creativity and restitution sit right next to each other."[6] The manifesto was published in part in a 1971 issue of *Artforum*, but the Whitney Museum ultimately turned down her proposal.

Ukeles found an outlet for her ideas in a series of Maintenance Art Performances at the Wadsworth Atheneum in Hartford, Connecticut. For these pieces, she maintained the interior and exterior of the building, secured the galleries, and cleaned the displays.

The first performance, *Transfer: The Maintenance of the Art Object*, not only exhibited maintenance as art but also explicitly critiqued the museum's social structures that determine the relationship between art and maintenance. Ukeles selected a case containing a female mummy that would normally be cleaned by a maintenance person. As a "maintenance artist," Ukeles cleaned the case and stamped it with her signature, making it a piece of maintenance art and then putting a museum conservator in charge of its cleaning. By the simple act of the maintenance artist performing an everyday task—a task marked by her signature—the cultural value of the object is changed. Through this act Ukeles slyly subverts cultural norms. She makes clear that labor done by this workforce, though essential, is entirely undervalued.

Her next performance, *Keeping of the Keys*, turned attention toward maintenance as a defensive practice. Ukeles locked the entrances to the museum and each of the galleries for set amounts of time during its regular opening hours. Her actions conveyed the message that museum maintenance serves to protect the life of the objects contained therein, and indicated the power of the maintenance worker to control and manipulate large institutions like the Wadsworth Atheneum.

The last two performances, *Hartford Wash: Washing, Tracks, Maintenance: Inside* and *Hartford Wash: Washing, Tracks, Maintenance: Outside*, saw Ukeles conducting traditional maintenance tasks like scrubbing and mopping places where people walked. She cleaned largely by hand and, in the process, captured the physical difficulty of translating the tasks of maintenance to a large scale. She created an obvious discrepancy between the means of maintenance and the object being maintained, highlighting the private nature of maintenance through its uncanny appearance in public space.

On Maintenance

The fact is that street cleaners are welcomed like angels, and their task
of removing the residue of yesterday's existence is surrounded by
a respectful silence, like a ritual that inspires devotion, perhaps only
because once things have been cast off nobody wants to have to
think about them further.
  Nobody wonders where, each day, they carry their load of refuse.
Outside the city, surely; but each year the city expands, and the street
cleaners have to fall farther back. The bulk of the outflow increases and
the piles rise higher, become stratified, extend over a wider perimeter.
Italo Calvino, *Invisible Cities*[7]

69

Maintenance is a public act, not a private one, and the perceived distance between the architect and the public maintenance worker is much
greater than the reality. Large-scale, public maintenance practices have
become professionalized, and maintenance workers tend to be viewed
as a necessary service. The architect, alongside the client and the developer, predetermines the type of work and labor performance required.

Contemporary artists are concerned with issues of maintenance,
maybe more so than architects; this concern reflects their interest in
the real and the representational, and the collapse of these two worlds
into one reproduction or project. In her essay "Styles of Radical Will,"
critic Susan Sontag writes: "The systematic violation of older formal
conventions practiced by modern artists gives their work a certain aura
of the unspeakable—for instance, as the audience uneasily senses the
negative presence of what else could be, but isn't being, said."[8] Artists
give an oddly uncomfortable portrait of maintenance, increasingly
affirming the irony of the modern project. This portrait undoes and
unnerves architectural discourse.

To discuss the subject of maintenance forces us to question architecture as a singular, formalized, and fixed object. Architecture is a receiver
of weather, nature, and elements, whose factors constantly change
its properties. Even as architecture remains vertical or standing, it is
changed in perpetuity. Clean-looking buildings are a social commodity,
and architecture is generally considered a luxury. The inability to make
visible acts of maintenance is thus a failure of architecture.

Cleaning and the Politics of Labor

2.3

Mierle Laderman Ukeles, *Hartford Wash: Washing, Tracks, Maintenance: Outside*, 1973. Image courtesy of Ronald Feldman Fine Arts, New York.

LONDON'S NIGHTLY CLEANSING : SCENE AT THE BASE OF THE MONUMENT

The flashlight lets the camera see a picture of London life usually reserved for the reveller late returning, so far as the general public is concerned. All main thoroughfares receive a violent purging by water every night. At about 2 a.m. hoses are fitted to the hydrants, and men in oilskin aprons wash the day's filth into the gutter. The neighbourhood of Billingsgate, where this photograph was taken, is notoriously unsavoury, but these ministrations keep the " fish-like smell " from becoming too " ancient."

821

2.4

Cleaning the streets of Billingsgate,
twentieth century. Image courtesy
of Yale Center for British Art.

If, as Calvino says, the maintenance worker's "existence is sur-rounded by a respectful silence," it is possible to imagine a cold kind of silence that makes up the space surrounding the window washer—particularly further up, away from the street. Not only silence, but stillness.

The notion that humans have to exert enormous amounts of effort to scale and clean buildings produces a perverse landscape much akin to Sontag's discussions of pornography: the "fantastic enlargements of human energy are rather the ingredients of another kind of litera-ture, founded on another ... of consciousness."[9] According to this logic, maintenance belongs not only to architecture but also to social affairs, psychology, metaphysics, and so on. It offers the desire to enter other worlds—in strangers' homes or at great heights.

Architecture can be dishonest.
Maintenance is obscene.
Maintenance renders architecture conventional.
Maintenance is love.
Maintenance is beyond love.
Maintenance is a consciousness.
Maintenance is fulfillment.
Maintenance is agony.
Maintenance has power over architecture.
Architecture has little power over maintenance.
Maintenance confronts different scales.
Maintenance represents architecture.
Maintenance contradicts architecture.
Fineness is maintenance.

2.5

Window cleaners on the glass roof of the
Crystal Palace, London. Photograph,
June 2, 1933. Photograph by Imagno/
Getty Images.

Crystal Palace, Sir Joseph Paxton, 1851

The Crystal Palace was the first modern building to have its construction photographed from start to finish.[10] "In this black-and-white photo, men in harnesses are cleaning the expansive and glass-roofed arcade like building. ... The Crystal Palace, more cathedral than palace in scale, is among the first modern buildings that was a 'city-building,' a building built as a response to a 'city of calculation, filled with specificity.'"[11] This building followed not on Paxton's expertise as an architect or engineer, for he was neither, but as a gardener and conservatory builder, most notably for the Victoria regia glasshouse at Chatsworth (1850). In *The Architecture of the Well-Tempered Environment*, Banham writes of Paxton's greenhouse at Chatsworth: "Few buildings discussed in this book so far are comparable in terms of environmental ingenuity and performance with Paxton's house ... judiciously metering temperature, moisture and carbon dioxide levels in the atmosphere around his out-of-season chrysanthemums, he has more environmental knowledge at his fingertips than most architects ever learn."[12] The Crystal Palace, for which glass and iron are the primary building materials, through its transparent windows produced an immediate relationship of observation from both inside and outside. The use of glass on such a large scale is also understood as an "intermingling of rationalist and antirationalist impulses."[13] Figure 2.5 depicts window washers traversing the Palace's glass roof as a new performative surface to act upon. While the focus had been on the interior, the Palace's roof—a transparent, prefabricated structure—revealed a new social construct: the window washer *en masse.* It was necessary to organize a group of workers who would work together and scale the building. At the time of the Crystal Palace's completion, in 1851, the City of London was also introducing new organized labor to clean the streets. It is interesting to note not only the labor force needed on each of these projects, but the fact that each was made visible here for the first time.[14]

"WHITE WINGS" WHO HAVE NOT STRUCK

White Wings, Department of Street Cleaning, New York, 1930

Cleanliness is a national virtue in America. No filth, no dust.
Le Corbusier, *When the Cathedrals Were White* [15]

In New York you have to clean so much, and when you're finished,
it's not-dirty. In Europe people clean so much, and when they're
finished, it's not just not-dirty, it's clean.
Andy Warhol, *The Philosophy of Andy Warhol* [16]

Public maintenance originated in parallel with the development of cities. In 1850s London, a city booming with new infrastructures, a new class arose to maintain these new systems. Initially, street sweepers, often poor children or the homeless, would sweep the streets as others crossed in exchange for a bit of money. What began as an informal act shifted and changed as the city grew, developing paved roads and more permanent infrastructures. The sweepers were replaced with broom-equipped horse-drawn carriages, and the streets were hosed off at night to keep them clean. From an array of disorganized and ad hoc individual cleaners, an organized labor force developed to maintain the city, representing its growth and progress.

New York City experienced a similar progression. In 1895, George E. Waring, the city's street commissioner, created an organized group of uniformed street sweepers called the White Wings. Named for their all-white uniforms (which were required until the 1930s), the White Wings were part of an important effort to clean up the city. Their uniforms made them instantly recognizable, with the dual intention of advertising the city's cleanup efforts and discouraging workers from slacking on the job.[17] They would march together in parades, and the image of their collectivity was meant to be reassuring. Waring had provided the city with a new kind of army, one that could combat urban filth.

Today, the city's Business Improvement Districts (BIDs) hire maintenance workers not unlike the White Wings to maintain the streets, to prevent crime by acting as "eyes on the street," and to assist tourists or visitors with directions. Their uniforms are labeled with the name of their district.

2.7
Henri Sauvage, 26 Rue Vavin, Paris, 1912.
Photograph by Patrick Charpiat, taken
2007, licensed under Creative Commons.

Flats at Rue des Amiraux, Henri Sauvage, 1925

Influenced by recent construction techniques and use of contemporary building materials, the French architect Henri Sauvage used white Paris Metro tiles in covering the exteriors of his large-scale apartment buildings. These tiles, so crisp and white, lined the facades of the tiered-balcony apartment buildings designed and erected as part of the program for low-cost social housing known as HBM (Habitation à Bon Marché). In projects like Rue des Amiraux, these mostly white-tiled facades with deep-blue accents encased larger-scale floor plans for housing whose interior floor plates opened up to cavernous voids at the heart of the building. The bottom of this building section contains a hollowed space to be filled with social programming—in this case a likewise tiled swimming pool and deck.

2.8
Studio Piano and Rogers, Centre
Pompidou, competition drawing, 1971.
Image courtesy of the architects,
© Fondazione Renzo Piano.

Centre Pompidou Competition, Renzo Piano and Richard Rogers, 1977

If one looks closely enough at the competition drawings for the Centre Pompidou—through the diagonal structural framing, the cantilevered escalators, the transparent elevators, the media projections and billboard signage, and the rooftop antennae—it is possible to discern two window-washing rigs: one descended a quarter of the way down the facade, the other suspended at the top of the roof. In response to the competition brief, the architects intervened through design at two disparate scales: the first, at the urban scale, gave a visual presence to the museum within the dense fabric of the city; the second allowed unimpeded movement from the city to the space of the gallery.[18] Since it was a competition, working within the required medium of the architectural drawing was the place to articulate these two disparate scales and a vision for the intersection between people, technology, and art in architecture. The architects' concern with representing life through technological advances in devices and gadgetry became elements of their architecture. The design demonstrated a contemporary concern with the representation of life as much as with the representation of an art museum. Drawing building systems as architectural elements, by literally bringing those elements to the surface of the building rather than hiding them deep within it, created a new type of building where art and life commingled. Even maintenance was exposed.

2.9–2.11 (above and following pages)
Mies van der Rohe, Neue Nationalgalerie,
Berlin, 1968. Photographs by the author.

Neue Nationalgalerie, Ludwig Mies van der Rohe, 1968

Today, the Neue Nationalgalerie is in need of renovation and repairs. The building is famous for its novel construction whereby the roof—a structural welded frame—was put together on the ground and raised into place with minimal supports below. To complete the volume, large infill plate-glass panels were installed at the perimeter enclosing it. The building suffered problems of condensation on the windowpanes, producing a "condensation view": "the context oscillates between clear panorama and milky blur."[19] In this recent photograph, the glass has been shattered and a maroonish-red sealant holds it in place, protecting it from further splintering and failure. It is in this moment of breakage that transparency and reflection are lost. The window becomes opaque and weak. The slightest alteration to the profile will seemingly undo the attitude of less is more. What was once, for Mies, complete freedom of experimentation becomes, in the renovation, a precision game of careful calibration of parts. The realm of freedom and experimentation is perhaps less important to the reimagining of the whole image. It is not possible to just seal it up; it has to be mastered in the Heideggerian sense: "so long as we represent technology as an instrument, we remain transfixed in the will to master it."[20]

Cleaning and the Politics of Labor

2.12
Iñigo Manglano-Ovalle, *Le Baiser/
The Kiss*, 1999, video still, single
channel video installation with aluminum
channel structure, 12-minute loop.
Courtesy of the artist.

Desire

Cleanliness is driven by desire, and, according to Jacques Lacan, all desire is fundamentally directed toward the Other.[21] In the classic example, the child desires that the mother desire him. Translated into architecture, the client desires that the building desire her—architecture should yearn to be consumed. In order to prolong this relationship between client and building, another desire must enter into the relationship: one for architectural renewal. The maintenance worker, it follows, should desire this process of architectural revitalization, whether directly or as an extension of the architect, client, or society at large. But this desire is, inevitably, always incomplete.

As Lacan would point out, once the child realizes he is separate from the mother, an unbridgeable chasm opens up. Likewise, when the architect produces a building, there is always a gap between its idealized representations and the building itself—a gap that only widens with time through consumption, daily use, and decay caused by the elements. The consumer and the architect seek to close this void, to approach the building's original condition and to renew the erotic relationship of desire between the participant and the object. The cleaner enables this process and allows the two to enter into a symbiotic relationship, to be each other's desire.

Images of buildings seek to escape time altogether, to remain perfect. The architect and the consumer always look to hold on to this perfect object, but whereas the image is of utmost importance to the architect, the physical object is what matters most to the consumer. Cleaning, then, is an act held somewhere between the completion of the object and its unyielding consumption.

2.13
Iñigo Manglano-Ovalle, *Le Baiser/
The Kiss*, 1999, video still, single channel
video installation with aluminum
channel structure, 12-minute loop.
Courtesy of the artist.

Le Baiser/The Kiss, Iñigo Manglano-Ovalle, 1999

Perhaps the most obvious historical condition in the domestication of upkeep is the conception of the domestic as the domain of women, and of women as cleaners. This social condition is deeply rooted but flourished significantly in the nineteenth century and has been further encouraged by suburbanization. Iñigo Manglano-Ovalle calls particular attention to class and gender in his 1999 film *Le Baiser/The Kiss*, which broadens an existing body of work exploring the intersection between cleanliness and architecture as a critique of modernism.

In *Le Baiser/The Kiss*, a male window washer cleans Mies's Farnsworth House (1945–1951) while a female DJ stands inside, swaying to the music she is listening to on her headphones. Gender and social issues were an integral part of the Farnsworth House from the beginning, as Mies and his single female client, Dr. Edith Farnsworth, interacted as architect and client—and platonically as man and woman. Farnsworth, particularly concerned about the social pressures of marriage and family life to which she did not conform, found in Mies a friend and companion. His friendship provided relief from the lonely and unhappy period in which she had decided to build the weekend house as an escape from Chicago. However, in the years during and following the house's construction, the relationship between Mies and Farnsworth soured, turning into both a legal and a public battle over modernism; Mies remained attached to his vision while Farnsworth felt exploited. Farnsworth, and for that matter any occupant of the house, was meant to inhabit the building (and surrounding landscape) in accordance with Mies's intentions. In the case of Manglano-Ovalle's video, the DJ reminds us just how transparent the house is, and how much on display one could be in an all-glass house. It is also possible to see the DJ as a representative figure: she is female, but also alone, symbolizing Dr. Farnsworth's isolation from the rest of a society in which she may already have felt out of place.[22]

Manglano-Ovalle further explored this problem—of a person being an object on display in a modern transparent home—in his MASS MoCA installation *Gravity Is a Force to Be Reckoned With* (2009). In the exhibit

2.14
Iñigo Manglano-Ovalle, *Le Baiser/
The Kiss*, 1999, video still, single channel
video installation with aluminum
channel structure, 12-minute loop.
Courtesy of the artist.

Cleaning and the Politics of Labor

he references the Russian dystopian novel *We* by Yevgeny Zamyatin, quoting lines from the book such as: "I can see you now. I can see you banging your head on that glass wall you believe separates you from everyone else. That glass cube of yours that you hide in. Well I can see you, and don't be surprised if everyone else can see you."[23]

This blurring of domestic cleaning and maintenance deviates from the norm—a male figure cleans the house—and *Le Baiser/The Kiss* calls the viewer's attention to the social consequences of cleaning. The extreme transparency of Mies's glass makes the social structures even more clear. In this triad of artist, cleaner, and client, Manglano-Ovalle becomes the cleaner in the film, replacing Edith Farnsworth with the lone female DJ who is both in her element and on display. Mies is not present, but one cannot help but sense the lack of privacy and the importance of the architect's vision of the house, directing and controlling its occupants. Joan Ockman describes the end result of the relationship between architect and client as a "cruel breach of trust," in which Mies disregarded the client's desire for privacy, comfort, and budget.[24]

In the film, Manglano-Ovalle's window-washing is a way of establishing place. While Mies's minimal, transparent architecture gave Farnsworth, the house's owner and resident, no place to hide herself or her possessions, Manglano-Ovalle's actions seem to be, like the windows, completely indifferent to the woman inside; he is utterly consumed with cleaning the glass.

Seen alongside Manglano-Ovalle's other two video installations that engage with Mies's work—*Climate* (2007) and *In Ordinary Time* (2001)—*Le Baiser/The Kiss* clearly makes a political commentary about the architect and about vulnerability, even if the artist is fabricating the facts. We could see Manglano-Ovalle as art critic Pamela Allara does, as a "slave to modernist beauty," but his actions also express something more hopeful: a connection to the architecture.[25] As a window washer, he "kisses" with the squeegee, which produces kissing sounds as he runs it across the glass.

Manglano-Ovalle is not simply making a pessimistic commentary on isolation; neither is *Le Baiser/The Kiss* simply ironic, or an attempt to make critique more enjoyable and accessible. The glass plane, although clear, acts as a barrier (metaphorical and physical) between two people of different classes. But instead of reading the project solely as a commentary on the dehumanization of labor, we see Manglano-Ovalle making something present to the viewer that modernism has tried to render absent.

The DJ is absorbed by her music in the house that renders all her actions public (the voyeurism that Dr. Farnsworth hated). She has become immune to those on the outside, and those on the outside have no influence on her actions. Her house remains, almost mystically, eternally new.

Furthermore, the maintenance worker becomes the person who knows the house, who knows how to love it—how to kiss it—even though he does not inhabit it. The cleaner remakes the world and reinvigorates desire: the object's desire for the client and the client's desire for the object. Manglano-Ovalle kisses the house, pointing out its failures and shortcomings but also renewing a relationship that modernism suppressed. The Farnsworth House must admit that it is incomplete, desirous of Manglano-Ovalle's love.

He captures this desire again in his later film, *Always After* (2006), in which the glass walls at Mies's Crown Hall are broken and an anonymous figure sweeps up the shattered pieces of glass. Even in the midst of the building's destruction, the film captures the desire to give order to these pieces of broken glass, which could be seen as remnants of a failed or incomplete modernism in the face of advanced, contemporary technology. Here, through these films, maintenance is depicted as a force of life that sustains people, objects, and their relationships.

7/10   Marcel Duchamp   Man Ray 1/20

3

VISUALIZING DECAY

Maintenance, while largely underrepresented in modern and contemporary architectural discourse, has a striking and notable presence within art and art discourse. Since the 1970s artists such as Mierle Laderman Ukeles and Gordon Matta-Clark have brought issues of decay, damage, degradation, and disappearance to the fore. Through their work they have rendered visible an otherwise invisible problem, raising a number of concerns including gender politics, the invisibility of labor, permanence and preservation, and questions of the aesthetics of wear. More recent artists have been instrumental in expanding on the foundational themes of Ukeles and Matta-Clark by taking up issues of cleaning and maintenance, and by extension taking the image and representation of modern and contemporary architecture as their task. These artists have treated maintenance allegorically, as a subject to explore. By looking at maintenance through different lenses, their work suggests new approaches to thinking about time, history, materiality of buildings, and durability, as well as to the visualization of architecture.

3.1
Man Ray, *Dust Breeding*, 1920, printed ca.
1967, gelatin silver print, 23.9 × 30.4 cm.
Purchase, Photography in the Fine Arts
Gift, 1969, © 2015 Artists Rights Society
(ARS), New York.

3.2
Film still from *Koolhaas Houselife*, 2008.
A part of the Living Architectures film
series by Ila Bêka and Louise Lemoine.
Images courtesy of Bêka & Partners.

Koolhaas Houselife, Ila Bêka and Louise Lemoine, 2008

Koolhaas Houselife, filmed at Rem Koolhaas/OMA's Maison à Bordeaux, is a particularly conspicuous example of the challenges buildings often pose to domestic work. Ila Bêka and Louise Lemoine treat major works of contemporary architecture as a background for their films, which take place in and around these works. The filmmakers use the buildings to highlight life within, commingling the formal and the social.

Their films portray architecture through events, featuring some of the typical and mundane ways inhabitants engage with iconic buildings through acts like cleaning, polishing, repairing, and maintaining. Presenting contemporary architecture with all of its imperfections marks a significant ideological shift in representation. They eschew the fixed, flawless, unoccupied images of modernism for the messy reality of life. Bêka and Lemoine reintroduce the human body in an unscripted way through candid, off-the-cuff conversations with the people who live or work in the buildings they portray. By incorporating the body of the worker, their films valorize the repetitive tasks that contribute to architecture's lasting images.

Koolhaas/OMA designed the Maison à Bordeaux for the newspaper editor Jean-François Lemoine, who was confined to a wheelchair after a tragic car accident. Every aspect of the house was developed with him in mind, in order to improve his quality of life. Rather than treating his disability as a handicap, Koolhaas approached it as a design opportunity to explore new ways of living. However, Lemoine passed away in 2001, just three years after the building's completion. As an experimental house—a house unlike any other, its form and parts both unique and untried—this house has a paradoxical status. It is aging, like all buildings, and, as we see in the film, suffers leaks, normal weathering, and wear. The Maison à Bordeaux's iconic architectural status has made these problems all the more significant since the building has been listed for preservation in perpetuity.

In some ways the original house no longer exists, since it has required specific replacement of its pieces and parts. The rehabilitation work has even resulted in some new effects, like the repaired concrete spiral staircase, which is far rougher than the original. What does the aging of the building say about it as a work of architecture? Do these contingencies point to the ultimate shortcomings of architecture? If we change the way we conceptualize the future of buildings, we can allow for continued engagement between architect, maintenance worker, and inhabitant, where the maintenance worker is most perceptive about materials and durability.

Koolhaas Houselife portrays the housekeeper, Guadalupe Acedo, as a sort of mediator between architect and client. In domestic images of iconic architecture the client is typically featured, but here, in the Maison à Bordeaux, the cleaner becomes the focus of the film. This emphasis establishes her position within the house, and demonstrates not only that client and cleaner are two distinct users of the building, but that the cleaner has a completely different relationship to the building. The act of cleaning is separate from what we tend to think of as living in this intimate architectural context. Yet here cleaning becomes an allegory for living, and also for love.

The introductory frame of the film features Acedo standing with her mop and bucket on the elevator platform as it slowly rises from the cave level to the private floor above. As the primary caretaker of the Maison à Bordeaux, Acedo becomes the main character in the narrative. Sleeping in the staff quarters every weeknight, she explains that she spends more time at the Maison à Bordeaux than at her own home.

The second scene opens on the annual European Heritage Day, when all historic buildings are made accessible to the public. It is raining outside, and visitors are asked to remove their shoes, so as not to leave the house in a "bad state." It is at this moment that the context of the house and the significance of its historic status are revealed. The camera continues to follow Acedo, giving the viewer a sense of how long it takes to walk from room to room and climb the stairs through the house's three levels. All the while, Acedo subtly reflects the scenery in her burgundy apron, a similar color to the Maison's floating top floor, and her black-and-white polka-dot blouse, reminiscent of the portal windows on the façade.

In addition to this moving portrait, the filmmakers produced a book with screen captures and photographic stills of Acedo visiting window washers and the gardener at work. The book includes numerous drawings mapping her route through the house, reminiscent of Andy Warhol's *Dance Diagram* series (1962).[1] These drawings document her movement through and around the space of the architecture—movements that are both directed and purposeful, but also improvised in response to the house.

The Maison à Bordeaux is demanding in a way that is often comical, if not absurd. The poignancy of the film arises from the humor of the house's inhabitants and the situations they find themselves in, which Koolhaas describes as a meeting of "the platonic conception of cleaning with the platonic conception of architecture."[2]

When we watch Acedo clumsily climb the spiral staircase with vacuum cleaner, mop, and bucket in hand, the architecture takes on another set of implications. In an interview that accompanies the film, Koolhaas responds to this scene with a critique of the cleaning practices, not the architecture:

> I am kind of surprised by the fact that someone who has such a daily involvement [with the building] is so insistent on a kind of generic technique of cleaning something so exceptional. I can easily imagine if I were a cleaner—maybe this is something we should have thought of—[I would have devised] some sort of protocol of what is convenient to be done by hand and what is convenient to be done by machine. I am completely surprised that something that is as harsh and exceptional as the spiral staircase is treated with a Hoover. It is completely insane.[3]

His disappointment is not that the building gets dirty, or that the housekeeper is unduly burdened, but that his architecture has failed to inspire a particular kind of organization: that contemporary living could come undone through the most mundane of acts; that a kind of coherence and clarity of form, which is simplifying life, unravels through the cleaner. The presentation of the cleaner is in some respects a representation of a source of entropy within the house.

Creation and completion, like upkeep and the unfinished, are two opposing processes. As Koolhaas continues: "It is not necessarily daily life confronting an exceptional structure, it is two ideologies confronting one another."[4] Cleaning and architecture are not fixed categories; rather, they are two historically developed concepts continually winding around each other. However, along with Koolhaas, we may also say that maintenance stands in opposition to an architecture that sees itself as organizationally clear and conceptually diagrammatic. In other words, there is no room for mess. Cleaning remains separate from the house, unable to fully integrate its unique requirements.

The two Platonic systems of cleaning and architecture are pure and reified. First there is the architectural object: new and complete. In a telling exchange in the film, the interviewer asks Acedo whether the building is complete.

Interviewer: It's leaking because the works are not over [*sic*]? Isn't it?
Guadalupe: Exactly! Everything is halfway done!
Interviewer: The house or the glass?
Guadalupe: No, the glass! The house is fine!
Interviewer: The house isn't halfway done, is it?
Guadalupe: No, the house is fully done!

For her, the architecture is separate from its cleaning. Maintenance becomes its own ideal system, permanently opposed to architecture—it has its own history, its own domain. This opposition at the Maison à Bordeaux is not everyday cleaning versus extraordinary architecture, but architectural thought versus cleaning, whereby an organized system, thoroughly planned, would be more in alignment with the architect's thoughts. And yet, it is possible to argue that the house is a more real version of itself by virtue of having gone through its daily upkeep and cleaning. It is here that Acedo's love for the house is on display.

If maintenance and architecture are characterized as independent, we run into the danger of failing to understand maintenance altogether. Maintenance is not a separate process to be juxtaposed with the finished building; it is a constant act of becoming that necessarily relates to the architectural object. Architecture and maintenance are inherently interdependent.

Madeness

Imagine a house where no cleaning is ever done. Dirty dishes pile up, windows get clouded with dirt, the carpet becomes matted, and equipment ceases to function—cleanliness and intended form are lost. Natural forces destabilize order and cause materials to decay—roots invade pipes, rust corrodes metal, weather attacks finishes.

The task of someone who cleans is to maintain objects—in this case, architecture—for repeated use. Cleaning, unlike restoration, reconstruction, or rebuilding, temporarily preserves the quality of an object's making, its *madeness*.[5] We tend to think more about what objects do than how they are put together, and "madeness" is the attribute that calls our attention to this dichotomy. Objects created to fight off nature's wear and tear reflect the knowledge and ideological usefulness of their design.

The architect operates in the conceptual realm of ideas that may (or may not) be made manifest in a finished building.[6] When buildings are constructed, complete, and occupied, the architect's intentionality and preestablished order inevitably confront the post-occupancy contingencies of use and everyday life.

Enter the cleaner. Guadalupe Acedo's work at the Maison à Bordeaux ensures the continued use of the house *and* its perpetual experience. The act of cleaning continuously returns the house to its original condition (or at least aspires to). This manual upkeep, which is not maintenance, extends the building's cycle of use, as order is alternately regained and lost. Acedo makes the house new again—a creative act in its own right. Perhaps she is also making it a better version of itself, by the sheer repetitive nature of acts of cleaning and taking care.

3.3 (following pages)
OMA's Maison à Bordeaux was declared
a Historic Building within three years
of its completion. Venice Biennale, 2010.
Photograph by Hans Werlemann,
courtesy of OMA.

3.4

Film still from *Gehry's Vertigo*, 2013. A part of the Living Architectures film series by Ila Bêka and Louise Lemoine, featuring the Guggenheim Museum, Bilbao, by Frank Gehry. Image courtesy of Bêka & Partners.

Visualizing Decay

Cleaning is neither the pure, individual creation of the architect nor the pleasurable consumption of the user; as a result, architectural culture undervalues it. Maintenance, however, is essential to the functioning of society and should be understood as critical to the life of architecture. Cleaners are the mediators between architects, buildings, and their users.

Morning Cleaning, Jeff Wall, 1999

Artist Jeff Wall's *Morning Cleaning* is an approximately eleven-by-six-foot illuminated color photo of the infamous Barcelona Pavilion for the International Exposition in Barcelona, designed by Mies van der Rohe in 1929. The photograph mimics the composition of widely distributed historic images of the building, but the strange lighting, the depiction of the window washer, the suds on the glass, his jacket on the chair, evoke something unfamiliar about the otherwise well-known scene.

The Pavilion was disassembled when the show closed in 1930. Its architectural significance, however, led to its reconstruction in 1986. Notable for its open plan, its precise and luxurious surface treatments, and its spatial complexity, the Pavilion is a structure of clean lines and rigid geometries, minimally furnished.

Hardly any historical photographs show people in the Pavilion, and, as Rolf Lauter points out, this makes the presence of the cleaner all the more jarring: "Wall thus fills a unique item of architecture with individual life and strips it of its special aura as an historical architectural monument."[7] Wall's image draws our attention to a hidden side of the Barcelona Pavilion. It makes evident the unseen work of preserving both the building and its images. He disrupts history, image, and sensibility to acknowledge the mundane task of daily upkeep, thereby revealing a certain reality and truth.[8] He undoes the history of the building as a fixed view. Even if it is fake or a fiction, it nonetheless challenges both the architecture and the photograph. It constructs a competition. Does this new image supersede the original? Does it take over? Both present realities of the building, and both are real images of the building. But one is closer to handcraft—the janitor who literally brings his hand up against the architecture.

Technology in this case enables the architecture to be scrutinized not only by the act of cleaning but also by photography. Wall's other work *Diagonal Composition No. 3* (2000) shows a close-up of a corner of dirty wall and chipped linoleum floor with a mop and a dirty bucket of water—another reality radically different from the luxury and organization that are expected from Mies.

3.5

Jeff Wall, *Morning Cleaning* (detail), Mies van der Rohe
Foundation, Barcelona, 1999, transparency in light box,
204 × 365 cm. Kunstsammlung Nordrhein-Westfalen.
Image courtesy of Jeff Wall. The nonpublic act of
cleaning represents a disruption in the interior of the
Barcelona Pavilion.

Visualizing Decay

Conical Intersect, Gordon Matta-Clark, 1975

In 1975, the American artist Gordon Matta-Clark (1943–1978) executed *Conical Intersect*, one of his well-known "building cuts," in two seventeenth-century buildings slated for demolition in central Paris. The site had been chosen for the future Centre Pompidou, designed by architects Renzo Piano and Richard Rogers. In an interview Matta-Clark referred to architecture's status as a "maintenance issue," declaring that built architecture presents a problem of maintenance over form.

> The very real nature of my work with buildings takes issue with a functionalist attitude to the extent that this kind of self-righteous vocational responsibility has failed to question, or reexamine, the quality of life being served. I know that this may sound like an artistic rationalization (and to some extent it is), but it is exactly here that I defend Art against Architecture—or at least that aspect of Architecture that is a janitor to civilization. I don't mean to belittle the janitor's role as people, only as policy.[9]

Interestingly, his art speaks more to the process and techniques of deconstruction than to preservation. Matta-Clark's projects were significant for the way they cut buildings, dividing houses in half and slicing complex geometric shapes out of abandoned structures that were about to be demolished. Maintenance would hardly seem to be of concern to his work, considering that the buildings he worked in were all going to be torn down. But within all of these structures, Matta-Clark observed architecture's decay—its failings over time, the apparent end of its social or cultural significance.

3.6

Gordon Matta-Clark, *Conical Intersect*, 1975, photomontage of two gelatin silver prints, 17.1 × 14.5 cm. Collection Centre Canadien d'Architecture/Canadian Centre for Architecture, Montreal, Gift of Estate of Gordon Matta-Clark. © 2015 Estate of Gordon Matta-Clark / Artists Rights Society (ARS), New York.

Matta-Clark criticized functionalists for justifying their work without a careful consideration of the spaces they made. He would often be the last person to occupy a building. His process was not refined—he carved his openings with hammers, chisels, and bow saws. Architecture's inevitable obsolescence, selective demolition, and transformation brought him closer than most architects to the problems of buildings. In this way he could experience architecture in the raw, its demolition as part of a long history of urban destruction.

Architecture has frequently positioned form against different environments—social, cultural, or climatic. Platonic ideals that had long been fundamental tenets of design practice have recently given way to a diverse array of design strategies that engage the progression of time through the transmogrification of stable geometries into geometries of instability. While this does reflect an important rethinking, discourse remains limited within architecture. The actual life of architecture—its enduring presence in time, its environment, its users, and its intersection with maintenance—have gone largely undocumented and unconsidered within architectural discourse, specifically in regard to public acts.

Matta-Clark's work offers an approach for architects to begin to address these issues by setting up the problem of architecture versus sculpture. His cuts, captured through film and photography, present a clear and striking position on the relationships between architecture, maintenance, and site. Their potent and lasting images still stir the imagination and remain a provocation to architecture's worth. Matta-Clark's elegant but brute-force deconstructions parallel an emerging repositioning of architecture in relation to modernity as radical works of art.

Cleaning the Rietveld Pavilion, Job Koelewijn, 1992

In 1992 Job Koelewijn, a Dutch art student, completed his thesis, *Het schoonmaken van het Rietveldpavilijoen* (Cleaning the Rietveld Pavilion), for which he enlisted his mother and three aunts to wash the Pavilion by hand while wearing the traditional dress of Spakenburg, his hometown. Koelewijn's project is not just about cleaning as a measure of restoration but, as critics Carel Blotkamp and Sjoukje van der Meulen point out, is "a narrative about the everyday, cleanliness and beauty."[10]

The performance deals with the ritualistic nature of cleaning domestic living spaces, primarily the house, and speaks to Dutch Calvinist heritage. Cleansing the body, an object, or an area plays an important role in many religious rites. Traditionally speaking, "cleanliness is next to godliness," and Koelewijn seems to be saying so through his art.

This performance/action/event garnered him a place in the *Post-Nature* catalog for the Dutch Pavilion at the 2001 Venice Biennale. The catalog describes the project as "a recleansing of the idea of cleanness, the cleansing of a single utopia."[11] Blotkamp and van der Meulen also point out that the Dutch word for "cleaning," *schoon*, suggests that beautification is part of the process. They note: "*Schoon* has two meanings: the most common one is clean or pure, but it is also a somewhat old-fashioned term for beautiful or fine, often in an artistic sense (*schone kunsten* is comparable to the English 'fine arts')."[12] Indeed, Koelewijn has already suggested the kinship between cleaning and art by presenting it as a performance, as part of his thesis.

3.7 (following pages)
Job Koelewijn, *Cleaning the Rietveld Pavilion 16 March 1992*, photograph.
Image courtesy of Galerie Fons Welters.

Visualizing Decay

The one-story Rietveld Pavilion, with its steel frame and large expanses of glass, provides the setting for Koelewijn's ephemeral event. The contrast between the traditionally dressed women and the modern glass box is striking for the disparate histories it brings together. Cleaning establishes a connection between the social and utilitarian ideologies promoted by the Nieuwe Bouwen movement (known as the New Building movement in early modernism) in the Netherlands and the "soberness and functionality of Rietveld."[13]

Koelewijn captured the actions of the performers through a series of color photographs offering seven different views of the women sweeping the ground, washing the glass walls on ladders, and standing together at the completion of the cleaning in their aprons, smocks, and bonnets.

3.8
Job Koelewijn, *Cleaning the Rietveld Pavilion 16 March 1992*, photograph.
Image courtesy of Galerie Fons Welters.

An attendant book produced by the artist has few images and even fewer words, but one sentiment is clearly put forward: "A woman who cleans will not lose her morality."[14] The book was dedicated to the Dutch modernist architect Gerrit Rietveld (1888–1964), who designed the building between 1950 and 1964 (it was completed after his death). The Gerrit Rietveld Academie was his largest project, but he did not live to see its completion either.[15]

Rietveld's work reflects his ambition to make architecture coherent and unambiguous. In 1958, he wrote: "when we build we should never lose a sense of relativity and we should aim for soberness, but however we are building, it will only become real for us, only bring us joy, if that visual sense of space that we are offering to another as a gift while retaining it ourselves, is not broken up, but remains intact, transparent and above all, clear."[16] The pedagogy of the school from 1939 to 1960 was largely shaped by the functionalist and sociocritical ideas of De Stijl and the Bauhaus under the direction of the architect Mart Stam.[17] Rietveld had been one of the original founding members of the De Stijl movement, but he later left and aligned himself more closely to the Nieuwe Bouwen movement.

Koelewijn's project is a critique of architecture's functionalist principles and the social aspects of labor. The industrially produced glass and steel characteristic of the functionalist movement—typically seen as tough and rugged—are portrayed as light and delicate in *Cleaning the Rietveld Pavilion*. The costumed cleaners are almost redundant—they have no trouble keeping the Pavilion clean—but they establish an important visual opposition with the glass building.[18]

Three other projects by Koelewijn directly engage issues of maintenance. His *Cleaning Cloth* (1993) consisted of a cloth distributed in plastic packaging decorated with a drawing of a cleaner wiping Bruce Nauman's famous neon spiral, encircling the phrase "The true artist helps the world by revealing mystic truths."[19] In *Broken White* (2004) and *Untitled* (2001), Koelewijn covers the walls in baby powder and glue, creating an environment that speaks to the fragility of its surroundings and the relationship between the vernacular and modernity. Koelewijn's projects weave together references to acts of revitalization and purification, simultaneously spiritual and confrontational.[20]

Cleaning the Drapes, Martha Rosler, 1967–1972

In *Cleaning the Drapes*, Martha Rosler presents a constructed interior: a woman vacuuming her living room, hosing down the drapes that cover the central picture window. Seemingly so absorbed in her work that she is oblivious to anything else, the housewife goes about her daily routine without regard for the world around her. While her home is maintained to a level of social acceptance, the woman is totally absorbed in the trappings of her suburban house, oblivious to the war.

3.9

Job Koelewijn, *Broken White*, 1998–2010. Image courtesy of Galerie Fons Welters.

3.10

Martha Rosler, *Cleaning the Drapes*, from the series *House Beautiful: Bringing the War Home*, ca. 1967–1972, photomontage, printed 2011, 17 ⅝ × 23 ¾ in. (44 × 60.3 cm). The Museum of Modern Art, New York, Purchase and The Modern Women's Fund. Digital image, The Museum of Modern Art, New York/Scala, Florence.

3.11

Jorge Otero-Pailos peeling the latex off
the wall of the Doge's Palace for his
piece *Ethics of Dust*, 2009. Photograph by
Michele Nastas. Image courtesy of
the Museo Thyssen-Bornemisza.

Ethics of Dust, Jorge Otero-Pailos, 2009

Jorge Otero-Pailos's installation at the 2009 Venice Biennale, *Ethics of Dust*, is part of an ongoing, larger project to preserve the dust and pollution that collects on the surfaces of old historic buildings. Otero-Pailos cleans walls—in this case those of the Doge's Palace—by painting them with latex, waiting for it to dry, and then carefully peeling it off. In this way the original wall is cleaned and a cast of it is made out of its collected residue. With this technique, Otero-Pailos is able to isolate the layer of dust and exhibit it as separate from the original—now cleaned—wall. Traditional building preservation techniques overlook the significance of dust, and instead sweep it away in order to renew surfaces. *Ethics of Dust* suggests that we lose something of our shared history when dust and other effects of pollution are removed. Otero-Pailos says of the problem of preservation: "The question for me is how can we lower the guard of preservation, which is so much about guarding—protecting heritage—so that it becomes open to other interpretations of heritage that are not intra-disciplinary but that are extra-disciplinary and that come from art and architecture?"[21]

Otero-Pailos has now preserved the dust of several historic buildings around the world. In many ways his project references the work of nineteenth-century architects and conservators, who made casts of buildings from distant places in order to further study them from afar.[22] His projects lend new meaning to our traditional notions of both preservation and cleaning, through reworking the acts of each. He is literally remaking parts of the building, even if they become dusty again.

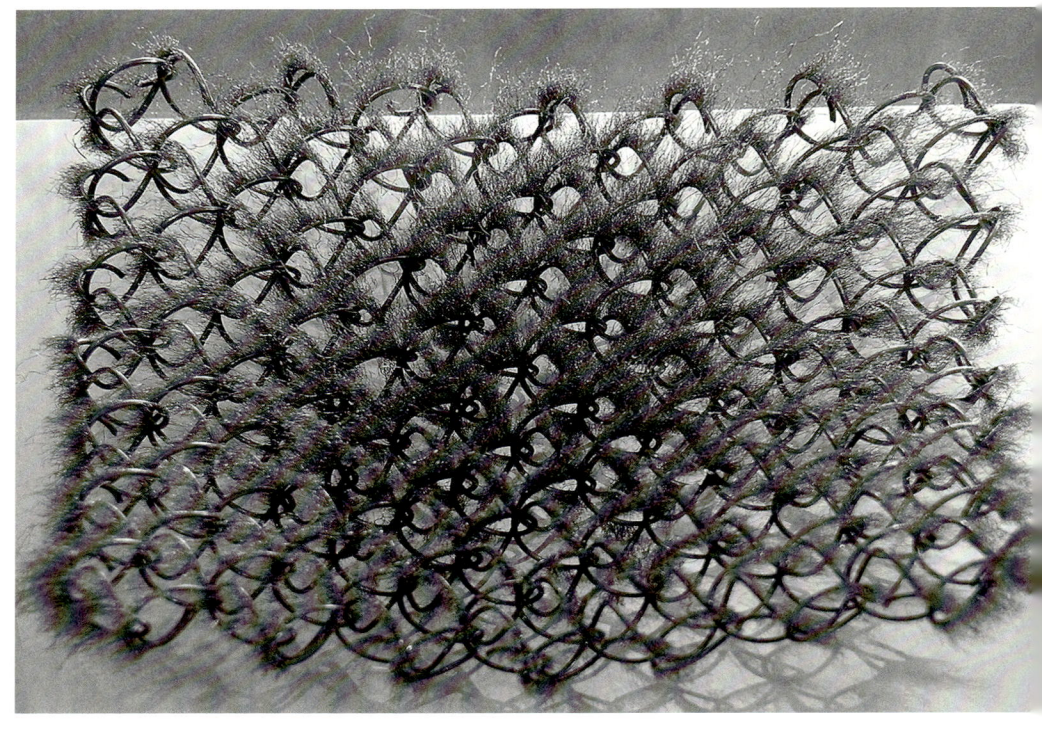

3.12
New-Territories/R&Sie(n),
Dust attraction by electrostatism,
Bangkok, 2002. Image courtesy
of the architect.

Dusty Relief, R&Sie(n), 2002

R&Sie(n)'s proposal for the Bangkok Art Museum, *Dusty Relief*, is a fuzzy form that encapsulates an unknown interior. Unlike other projects that approach themes of maintenance and cleanliness, this project is not white, sanitized, or hygienic; instead, it draws in dust and dirt. There is no hiding, no attempt to create a precious façade or employ titanium dioxide and other cellular technologies to remove deposits. *Dusty Relief* is sheathed in a chainmail-like metal mesh, as seen in the prototypes,[23] that *attracts* dirt and dust, conveying the message that the urban environment is eternally messy and unclean.

While the interior spaces "(white cube and labyrinth in a Euclidian geometry)" are not legible on the exterior "(dust relief on topologic geometry),"[24] the porous nature of the chainmail surface and stainless steel armature suggests that these spaces constitute a repository for an even denser collection of matter. This is not a white-box gallery interior but an accumulation of dirt particles and stuff held together by static electricity. It can be argued that it is a synthesis of durability through the toughness of material enclosure to capture waste, and that it produces an abstractly absurd form.

Although it is designed for the city of Bangkok, *Dusty Relief* could be found in any dense city. At first sight it looks dirty, worn, and aged. It is like an infrastructural building, an updated version of the type of building that contains or acts as a cleaning mechanism for the city, along the lines of McKim, Mead and White's Bronx Grit Chamber (1937).

The Bronx Grit Chamber is an early example of an urban facility created to clean urban water. A monument to New York City's urban renewal and its development toward a healthier and cleaner city, the Grit Chamber looks the part, with its classical brick-and-glass façade. Invisible from the street, the facilities sit underneath the building. It appears to be a small civic building, but its insides—its sewage treatment and water-cleaning system—are anything but white and hygienic.

Contemporary urban buildings have been passive recipients of connections, hookups, water pipes, and sewage outputs—the kinds of urban infrastructure supplied by the Grit Chamber. The Grit Chamber sorted particles larger than three-sixteenths of an inch, but nothing finer.

3.13
New-Territories/R&Sie(n), *Dusty Relief*,
Contemporary Art Museum, Pollution
Electrostatism scenario, Bangkok, 2002.
Image courtesy of the architect.

Chapter 3

Dusty Relief, however, acts as a much finer filtering device. Unlike the classical façade of the Grit Chamber, which hides and belies the dirty work of the structure beneath, here the building form exposes its dirtiness. Although it is a serious construction, it takes the curious form of a dust bunny. (Admittedly, the full-scale reality would be far less cute. Rain would make it soggy, damp, and smelly; wind would leave empty patches.) It produces a new kind of particulate matter in the city as it inhales urban dust, suggesting that the urban environment is making us all sick, that urbanism is unhealthy.

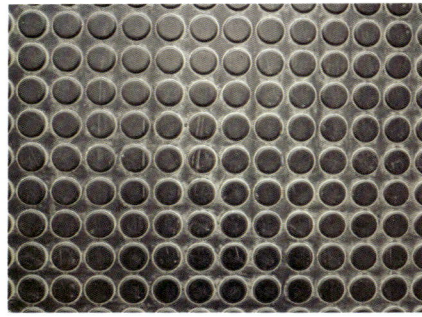

3.14–3.15

Rotor, *Usus/Usures*, 2010. Photographs
by the author.

Usus/Usures, Rotor, 2010

Rotor, a design collective based in Brussels, presented *Usus/Usures* (Uses and Users), an exhibition showcasing the material effects of usage, at the 2010 Venice Biennale. Installed at the Belgian Pavilion and displayed like a collection of minimalist artworks in the pristine gallery space, these architectural remnants index the peculiarities of their own wear. The pieces are provocative in the way they make actions legible through their trace, like a floor tile hung on a wall that reads as a map of the traffic of human feet.

Their *Blue Limestone Plinth* (2010) is a photograph of the blue limestone base of a building. The exterior wall is constructed of this durable stone to protect the building from wear—a traditional practice that can be seen in many of Belgium's public buildings. The catalog accompanying the exhibition comments on this photograph:

> No single person, regardless of their profession, can be a single repository of all the knowledge that must be woven into a specific situation. No designer can absorb all the phenomena which create a situation and be held as the sole person responsible for the resulting actions. Taking responsibility for one's actions—an idea we support—should not make the designer attempt omnipotence. Rather, experience has shown that knowledge of wear comes from recognizing the plurality of situated and anchored expertise acquired in particular by cleaning crews, maintenance managers and infrastructure managers. In the laboratory of reality, all these players are invisible and often underestimated researchers who contribute to sustaining a breeding ground of teaching and expertise, thus taking over from designers.[25]

Faced with a square of carpet that has a shape pressed into it, one can intuit the former presence of an appliance or a piece of furniture. Users are capable of projecting use onto surfaces, and vice versa. Rotor argues that "wear humanizes architecture and brings it to life."[26] Yet, throughout the history of modern architecture, ideas about the incorporation of cleaning and maintenance, or use and maintenance, have been repressed in favor of images that show architecture as perpetually new.

4

MODERNIZING MAINTENANCE

Over the course of the twentieth century, as new technologies emerged and cleaning processes became more streamlined, dreams of eliminating the labor of cleaning took hold. From traditional cleaning of the domestic setting to houses such as Buckminster Fuller's Dymaxion House and the Smithsons' House of the Future, which included mechanized washers and self-cleaning materials, the modern period saw a steady displacement of the human hand. The effects of this displacement are still unclear, and technological advances have yet to completely eliminate manual labor, but the legacy of these "maintenance-free" visions has been important in the formulation of contemporary discourse. We should now think critically about our current technologies in order to forge new paths forward.

With Robots, Diego Trujillo Pisanty, 2010

How we clean is one of the many ways we establish our individuality—that is, how we make our homes our own. The advent of domestic robots potentially puts this form of individuality in jeopardy, or at least radically alters it.

Diego Trujillo Pisanty's photographs of staged domestic scenes, *With Robots*, explore this possible future, illustrating how the home might change to accommodate robots. In Trujillo Pisanty's vision, items like flatware, sheets, and food become standardized and require bar codes for robots to read, follow instructions, and move throughout the house. When personal items become homogenized, the only area for expressing one's domestic personality might be in the efficiency of one's naming and labeling systems. What remains close to us is no longer the technical ability of an object or the object itself, but the data it produces. Through controlled organization, repeated on a daily basis, it is possible to find yet another meaning of endurance and the contemporary.

4.2–4.4
Diego Trujillo Pisanty, *With Robots*,
2010, digital C-prints, 24 × 16 in.
Images courtesy of the artist.

The Domestication of Cleanliness

When we think of *cleaning*, it is not the streets or the city that immediately come to mind, but the interior of the house and its contents. The daily activities of dirtying and then tidying our living space(s) are among the most basic engagements a person has with the world of objects and with the world through objects. The house we so often use without conscious consideration—walking from room to room, reading, talking on the phone, cooking, sleeping, sitting, and showering—suddenly becomes an object demanding our attention. The disheveled bed asks to have its sheets removed and washed, its pillows fluffed, and perhaps even its mattress flipped—all in order to have its dirt and disorder removed, to be restored. These actions are not exceptional, yet they both objectify and personalize the house.

The domestication of upkeep is a product not simply of individual experience but also of many historical developments that include everything from methods of plumbing to mechanized standardization and changing attitudes toward gender and class. These historical developments contribute to an understanding of our own subjectivity and the relationship between identity and a sense of place.

In *History of Shit*, psychoanalyst Dominique Laporte reflects on the increasing privatization of waste.[1] Waste has been thoroughly domesticated, neatly tucked away through the intricate weaving of pipes, the thick walls of building foundations, and sturdy connections to urban infrastructure in the ground. The Green movement has advanced this historical trajectory through things like the promotion of personal composting, but the phenomenological and political consequence of these advancements is an increasingly individualized subjectivity. In his introduction to Laporte's book, architect Rodolphe el-Khoury goes so far as to suggest that the individualization of waste has had a direct influence on the development of modern suburbs, and has created a sense of entitlement attached to the notion of private property. Laporte's account of history urges the reader to realize that neither maintenance nor its phenomenological experience is separate from its historical, hermeneutical development.

Modern architecture placed limitations on the subjective representation of buildings. The modern architect designed not only space but
also every aspect of a building's habitation. Because of the need to
uphold the building's image, maintenance work was rendered invisible.
To admit its importance would complicate the status of both the
architect and the owner.

The reality is that modern architecture requires constant maintenance, and the tools and techniques developed to reduce the time and
effort necessary for maintenance in modern buildings actually created
greater demands for care. Modern architecture isolates the necessary
practice of maintenance from buildings, rendering it obsolete and out of
place at the scale of the individual. It is this legacy of separation between
the traditional domestic cleaning of dwelling spaces and today's over-
whelming necessity to maintain large-scale urban buildings that
contemporary architects are now confronting. If we are to understand
this distinction, we must go back to early modern examples.

Befreites Wohnen, Sigfried Giedion, 1929

Modern architecture complicated the status of maintenance and cleaning with respect to the building. Because of its emphasis on style, materials, functionality, and efficiency, modern architecture made *newness* an ideological imperative. With this attitude, publications in the modern period, like architecture historian Sigfried Giedion's 1929 manifesto *Befreites Wohnen* (Living Liberated), bemoaned the problems of upkeep and functionality presented by the architecture of past eras. In his manifesto, Giedion proposes to combat this architectural inheritance with his list of ideas for "liberated living":

WE WANT TO BE LIBERATED FROM:
the house with eternal value
the house with expensive rent
the house with thick walls
the house as a monument
the house with high costs to enslave us
the house that exploits women as cheap labor.

INSTEAD WE NEED:
the cheap house
the open house
the house that makes our life easier.[2]

On the cover of the manifesto is a photograph showing a man leaning against a balcony rail and a woman leisurely seated in a chaise-longue. Spaces like this that incorporate expansive areas of glass, minimal detailing, and white walls are all forms of architectural liberation from the ornate buildings of the late nineteenth century.

Modern architecture demanded new protocols for more than just building, however. Modernism sought lifestyle change, and cleaning and revitalization suddenly became theoretically and rhetorically significant. Cleanliness embodied health, and because this new form of architecture promised to deliver a sanitary environment, it was believed to be better for the body. Modern architecture was even touted as having preventative qualities, furthering a feeling of good of health and aiding humankind in the fight against filth and disease in body and mind.

By collapsing the two standards of cleanliness and architecture into one, modernism altered the relationship between society and architecture. While architects have always been obsessive about their creations—from Vitruvius to Mies to the present—modernism passed a certain anxiety of upkeep on to its clientele. An idealized minimalism produced the demand for idealized upkeep. Around the mid-twentieth century, all kinds of cleaning products and technology went on the market to supply the demand and to facilitate this lifestyle.

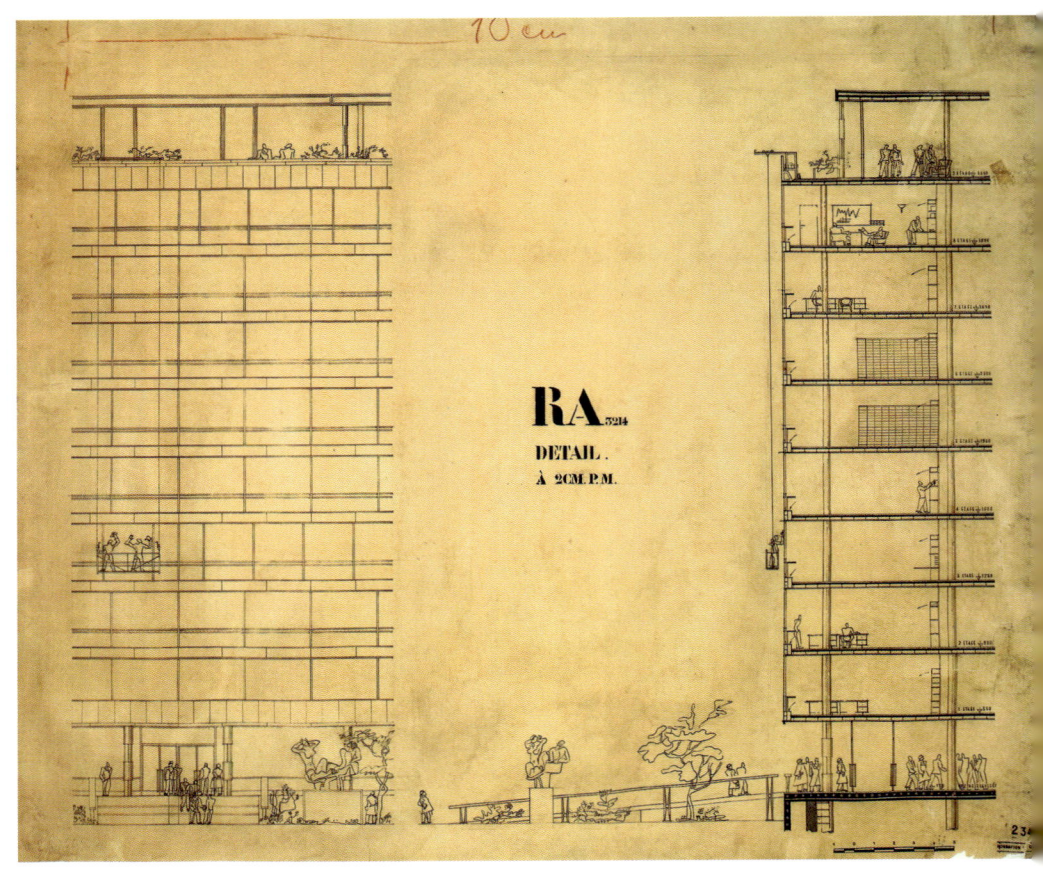

RA. 5214
DETAIL.
À 2CM. P.M.

4.5

Le Corbusier, Zurich, Immeuble
Rentenanstalt, 1933. Plan FLC 23466C,
© FLC/ARS, 2014.

Cité de Refuge, Le Corbusier, 1929

Le Corbusier is celebrated for thinking through technical problems, including maintenance, perhaps more than anyone else, for he thought about them in the early stages of a project, as illustrated in working plans where he draws in the window washer in the elevations and sections. He thought about the future requirements of keeping a building clean, maintained, and eternally new. Photographs of his Cité de Refuge include several that show the mechanism he designed to enable the window washers to do their work. (It had been thought that a hermetically sealed glazed window wall could regulate and maintain a particular kind of thermal interior environment, but the failure of the double glass wall has been recorded time and again in writings on this building.)

In a simple wall and building section of the design for his Rentenanstalt project for Zurich, he includes activities being performed on the interior of the building. The two-dimensional black-and-white drawings, with outlined people and furniture, are depictions of the kind of life that would be possible within. If one looks closely at the drawings, it is possible to distinguish two figures outside of the line that demarcates the building's enclosure, its weather wall. These two figures are men washing the newly completed glass wall. One is posed in what looks like the Modulor man configuration.

.

4.6 (left)

Le Corbusier, Armée du salut,
Cité de Refuge, Paris, 1929. Photographie
FLC L2(4)11, © FLC/ARS, 2014.

4.7 (top)

Le Corbusier, Armée du salut,
Cité de Refuge, Paris, 1929. Photographie
FLC L2(4)92–96, © FLC/ADAGP, 2014.

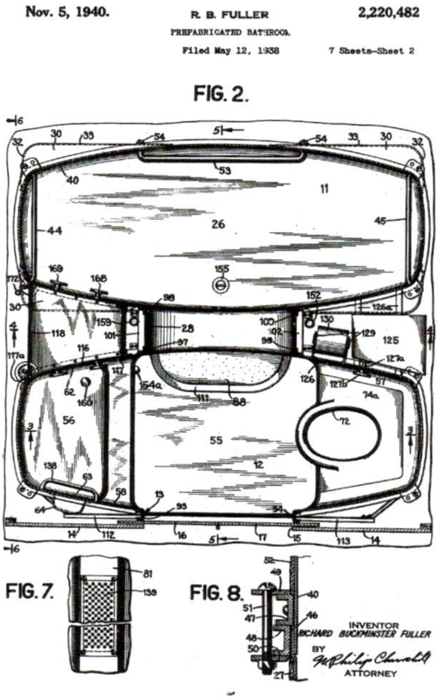

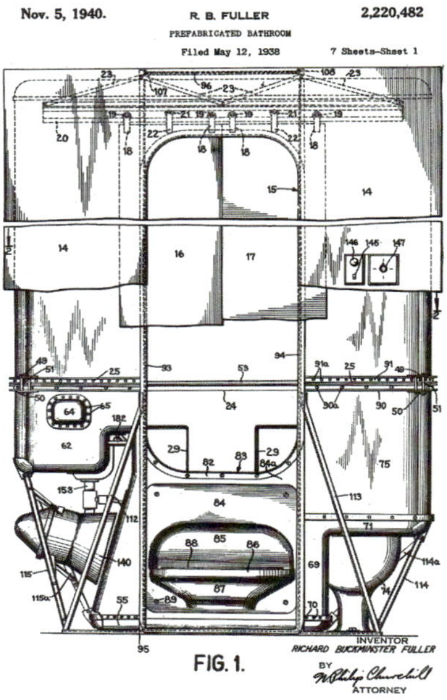

Nov. 5, 1940.   R. B. FULLER   2,220,482
PREFABRICATED BATHROOM.
Filed May 12, 1938   7 Sheets—Sheet 2

FIG. 2.

FIG. 7.   FIG. 8.

INVENTOR
RICHARD BUCKMINSTER FULLER
BY
ATTORNEY

Nov. 5, 1940.   R. B. FULLER   2,220,482
PREFABRICATED BATHROOM
Filed May 12, 1938   7 Sheets—Sheet 1

FIG. 1.

INVENTOR
RICHARD BUCKMINSTER FULLER
BY
ATTORNEY

4.8–4.9

Buckminster Fuller, Dymaxion
Bathroom, 1936. Courtesy of
The Estate of R. Buckminster Fuller.

The Dymaxion House, Buckminster Fuller, 1929

Beginning with his 4D houses, Buckminster Fuller eventually developed the hanging hexagonal shape into the more rounded Wichita Dymaxion House,[3] with its curved form and corners in lieu of straight edges to make a cleaner and maintenance-free house. In 1929 the house was exhibited at Fields Department Store as the centerpiece of a furniture display. Aside from its many structural and economic innovations, the Dymaxion House was made from materials that required minimal maintenance. It had a centralized vacuum and cleaning system designed to draw dust through cracks in the baseboards, where it was then filtered. Fans were carefully placed throughout to minimize odor and prevent the fogging up of glass. In short, the house was designed to clean itself.

Other architects, like Eileen Gray and Richard Neutra, showed a proclivity for home environments that, while functionalist and clean, were also humanist. However, while the International Style served as a unifying aesthetic and image, especially as a tool of capitalism, the Dymaxion House, along with a host of other futurist domestic inventions, never gained strong public appeal. If these experimental houses contained the potential for living a maintenance-free life, why did they fail to catch on? Perhaps because, as Mark Wigley writes, "in radicalizing every aspect of a house, it is no longer even recognizable as a house."[4] Fuller rejected the International Style, the dominant architectural movement at the time, as he believed it "demonstrated fashion-inoculation without necessary knowledge of the scientific fundamentals of structural mechanics and chemistry."[5] Unifying modernism under the banner of the "International Style," or any other moniker dependent on style, is often reductive and highly interpretive. Fuller's critique instead looked toward a scientific system of rationality.

Maintenance resulted from a history of subjectification that caused it to be conceived as a personal, domestic practice, yet now it is important for establishing a personal, domestic place. In addition to losing the semiotic and stylistic markers of home—a criticism voiced by the postmodern generation—modernist housing often assumed that

4.10
Buckminster Fuller, Dymaxion
Bathroom, 1936. Courtesy of
The Estate of R. Buckminster Fuller.

rationalization, efficiency, and self-sustaining architecture are ends in and of themselves. While they made for great exhibitions and great television, these houses never garnered mass-market appeal. Perhaps this is a reflection of the public's architectural conservatism, but it also seems that there is a general reluctance to let go of traditional maintenance practices. The maintenance-free house, particularly the stylistically minimal house, leaves no room for individuals to make their own environments.

Though maintenance is something people often complain about, it also allows us to make our homes our own. How can we explain the absurdity of perfectly mowed and edged lawns, carefully planted and mulched flowerbeds, and freshly painted houses, except as acts of *madeness*? The maintenance of a house is the maintenance of place, but there may be alternate ways of establishing place and alternate expressions of maintenance.

House of the Future, Alison and Peter Smithson, 1955–1956

Alison and Peter Smithson's House of the Future was presented in 1956 as part of the Daily Mail Ideal Home Exhibition in London. Designed to anticipate what domesticity would be like in the year 1981, the house was a compact but comfortable home for a childless couple, clean and free of clutter. Even the beds did not have blankets, as the house was to be kept at just the right temperature for sleeping.

Glamorous and futuristic, all the rooms in this house were made of continuous pieces of plastic whose curved geometries made them easy to clean. All of the house's appliances were fully integrated into these molded units, and the bathroom even featured a self-cleaning tub that filled from the bottom and washed itself with foamless detergent.

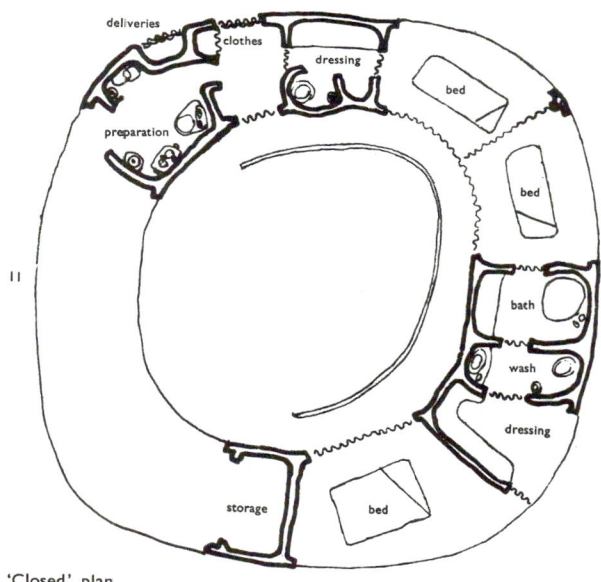

'Closed' plan

4.11

Alison and Peter Smithson, Appliance House, 1956. Alison and Peter Smithson Archive. Courtesy of the Frances Loeb Library, Harvard University Graduate School of Design.

Another important purifying feature of the house was its use of air-conditioning. As historian Beatriz Colomina points out in her essay "Unbreathed Air 1956," air conditioners were just starting to be advertised for domestic use at the time, and House of the Future incorporates them as a significant health feature that can even expel all smells and odors.[6] Upon entering the house, one could pass through an elaborate decontamination process whereby "a curtain of warm air" would remove all dust from the body.[7]

The House of the Future, however, was a bit of a hoax. Made of plywood, plaster, and paint, it was a simulation of plastic; the house functioned as an *image* of future standards of living rather than as an actual prototype.[8] Still, it is the house's function as an image that makes it so striking. Rather than accurately predicting what houses would be like in the 1980s, House of the Future speaks more precisely about attitudes and desires for maintenance in the 1950s. It projects a kind of modern obsession with health and leisure, and looks to liberate the housewife from domestic chores. Both the House of the Future and the quirky and odd Appliance House, which exists only as a freehand drawn plan, expand on ideas of how the insides of buildings work—setting aside the significance of the enclosure.

The Smithsons worked through problems of technology in a series of projects ranging from funny little bread houses to a snowball house. Figure 4.11 illustrates a series of rooms that are organized through their appliances and utility. Each room gains a purpose and a use. In this "closed plan," each bedroom is on the other side of what seems to be a curtain, drawn as a squiggly line to separate the innermost private spaces from other more functional ones. A corridor stops short and wraps in on itself, becoming an internal courtyard. Here, cleaning is thought of through the inclusion of contemporary appliances and the adoption of smooth and fluid surfaces that eliminate corners and dust. One might imagine the squiggly line that defines the curtain to be a thick, heavy, and sound-absorbing fabric that keeps out the noise of all those humming appliances. Likewise, the very thin lines between bedroom and bathroom would need to insulate from the sounds of water running, toilets flushing, and so on. These clean and distinct spaces produce conditions of noisy overlaps and layers of life within them.[9]

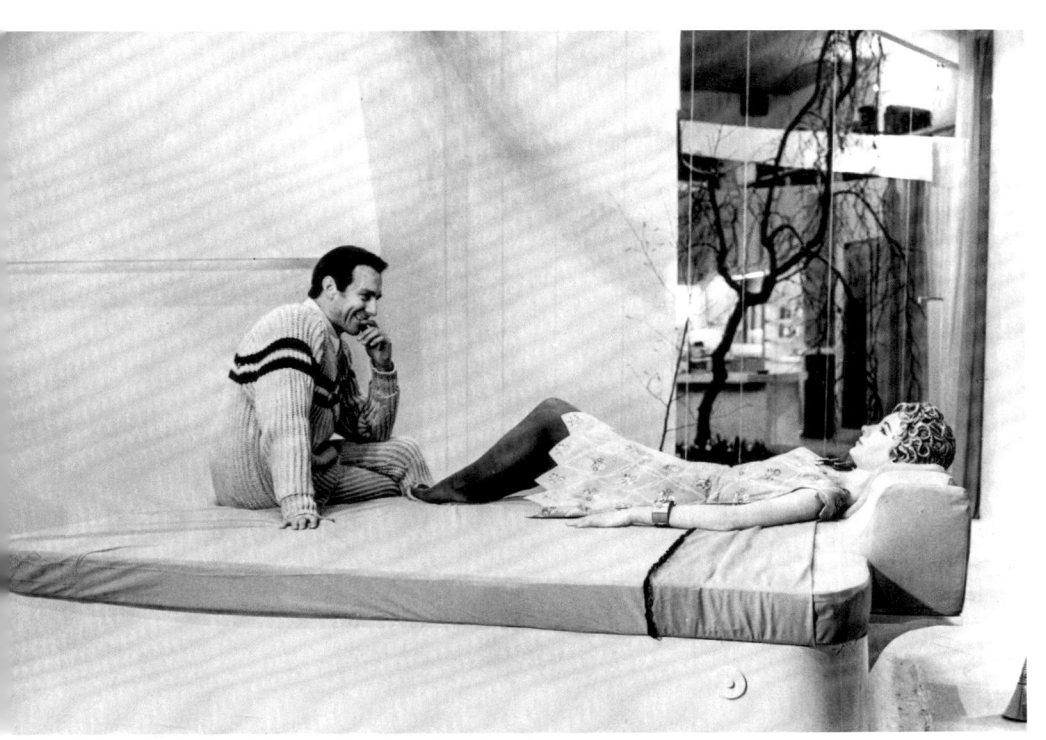

Modernizing Maintenance

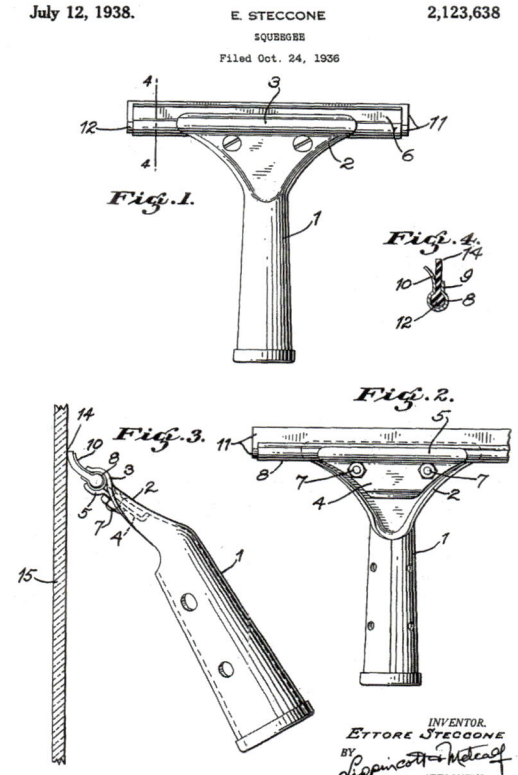

July 12, 1938.　　E. STECCONE　　2,123,638

SQUEEGEE

Filed Oct. 24, 1936

4.14

Ettore Steccone, Squeegee patent
drawing, 1938.

The Squeegee, Ettore Steccone, 1936

While it is rarely celebrated, the squeegee is one of the most important developments in the history of maintenance. Now a commonplace object, it can be situated within a collection of early technical inventions that were designed to reduce the physical effort and time spent on window maintenance. Although the routine task of cleaning glass windows with a squeegee was ultimately still mundane, it could now be executed more efficiently.

The revolutionary window squeegee, with its rubber blade edge and short handle, enabled effective glass cleaning, by hand, at different angles and different pressures.[10] It was designed by Ettore Steccone, an Italian immigrant living in Oakland, California; in 1936 he filed for a patent for it. A redesign of the "Chicago Squeegee," a heavy tool with two pink rubber blades held in place with twelve screws, it allowed windowpanes to be cleaned simply by unclipping the rubber blade from the lightweight brass body, avoiding the need to unscrew the blade connection.[11]

The squeegee enabled quick, precise work, requiring less time and resulting in a cleaner surface. The invention of the rubber blade impacted all kinds of glass cleaning, not just on buildings but on everything, from car and airplane windshields to lighthouses. It would even become an integral piece of equipment for artists. Gerhard Richter, for example, used the squeegee to apply paint, experimenting with the thickness of the paint and the effects that light has on varying layers. While the practical activity of applying paint is fundamentally different from removing dirt and dust, both should nevertheless be viewed as worldly transformations.

The razor-sharp rubber blade of the squeegee has a square edge, and the type of rubber is a "carefully guarded secret."[12] The squeegee is still manufactured by Ettore, a company that grosses $50 million, while their business has now extended to include other domestic and large-scale professional maintenance services.

A. DORMITZER.
CHAIR FOR WASHING WINDOWS.

No. 498,464. Patented May 30, 1893.

150

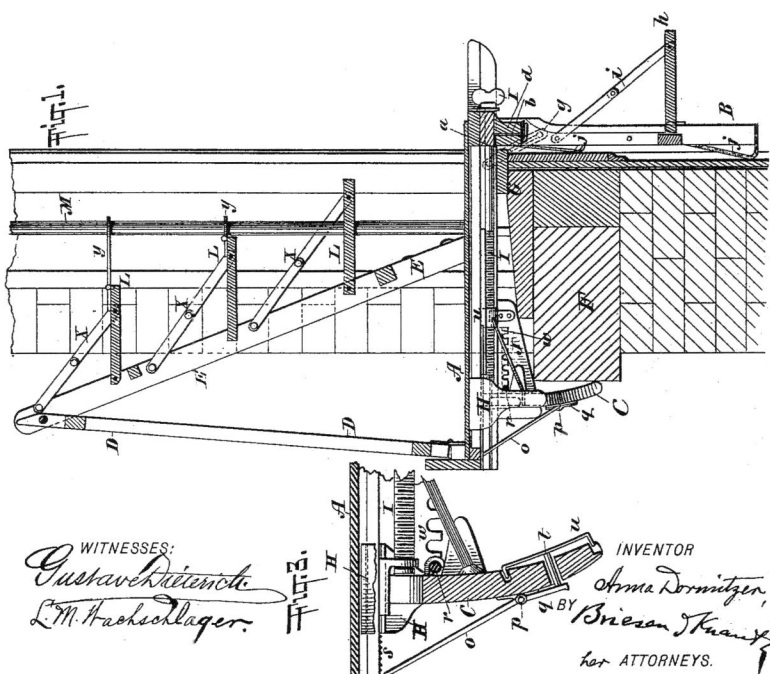

WITNESSES:
Gustave Dieterich
L. M. Hachschlager

INVENTOR
Anna Dormitzer,
BY Briesen & Knauth
her ATTORNEYS.

Window-Washing Chairs, Anna Dormitzer, from 1878

Novel inventions designed to clean domestic window glass were popular at the end of the nineteenth century. In fact, the number of women inventors who emerged at this time underscored the demand for products that made domestic tasks easier; washing double-hung windows, for instance, was both labor-intensive and unsafe. The New York City suffragist and patron Anna Dormitzer registered sixteen patents for a variety of window-washing devices, including chairs, stepladders, and a combination thereof.[13] The patents included precise line drawings of the devices and their detailing. Dormitzer not only offered solutions to the problem of cleaning windows, but also continued to refine her designs for more than ten years, demonstrating that cleaning was a serious business. Her technically successful Window-Cleaning Step-Chair (1878) combined a short stepladder with a seat on its top. It could be hung over a windowsill, thus allowing the homemaker to sit and clean the windows from the outside.[14] Glass would eventually stimulate aesthetic discourse around the idea of transparency, but Dormitzer's inventions signal another history, formed out of an increasing anxiety about the safety of cleaning windows and the amount of time needed for household upkeep. Her inventions were soon surpassed by other experimental devices, which further adapted earlier devices to produce new products, such as the Extensible Window-Washing Device (1906), which used metal "lazy tongs," a scrubber, and a hand crank to reach otherwise inaccessible window exteriors, and the Hydropneumatic Window-Cleaning Apparatus (1914), demonstrating that glass, for all its modern aesthetic and cultural allure, also led to technically adventurous solutions for its upkeep.[15]

4.15
Anna Dormitzer, Window-Washing Chair
patent drawing, 1893.

4.16
Self-cleaning glass, Pilkington
advertisement, 2001.

Self-Cleaning Glass, Pilkington Glass, 2001

Introduced to the market in 2001 by Pilkington Glass, self-cleaning glass was the first major innovation in glass products since the development of low-E coating in the 1980s.[16] Soon after its release other companies, like PPG (see chapter 1 above), developed competing but similar products.

The glass—Pilkington Activ™—has a coating that works in two stages: its photocatalytic properties use the sun to decompose dirt on the surface, while its hydrophilic components allow rain to spread evenly across the windowpane rather than form droplets, washing the loosened dirt away.[17] This combination significantly reduces the need for manual cleaning.

Self-cleaning glass has affected both domestic cleaning and public maintenance. The domestic effect is shown in a Pilkington advertisement (figure 4.16), where a woman stands at her front window looking out, her arms folded across her chest, signifying that she has time for relaxation and no longer needs to invest hours of labor in cleaning her windows. Where massive surfaces are concerned, however, the effect is totally different. These kinds of glass materials remove the working, human figure from the façade. This fortuitous development repositions the worker, effectively removing him or her from the surface of the building—not temporarily, but permanently. As a result, all images of work are removed from the building—not only the work done by humans, but also, potentially, that done by robots or any physical technological apparatus.

Workers wash the exterior of the National
Aquatics Center on November 10, 2008
in Beijing. The National Aquatics Center,
also known as the Water Cube, was
the venue for the swimming and diving
events during the Beijing 2008 Olympics.
Photograph by Cai Daizheng, 2008.

Beijing National Aquatics Center, PTW Architects, 2008

The Industrial Revolution's contribution to the great
cleanup can be understood under five rubrics: new goods,
new materials; dirt- and water-resistant surfaces;
water control and lighting.
Joseph Amato, *Dust: A History of the Small and the Invisible*[18]

The Beijing Water Cube, designed and built for the 2008 Olympics, has 155
a building skin made from ethylenetetrafluoroethylene (ETFE), a non-
stick, low-friction, and stain-resistant surface capable of spanning
greater expanses than glass. This chemically altered material, which
is normally invisible, has been rendered visible by Beijing's heavily
polluted air. The air quality proved less than amenable to the high-
performance translucent membrane, depositing excessive amounts
of grime on the otherwise postcard-ready façade.

With China's minimal labor costs and abundance of laborers, a low-
tech, less robotic or mechanized solution for cleaning the Water Cube
was chosen: a team of human window washers with handheld cleaning
equipment were individually suspended over the façade. This moment
was enthusiastically captured by the international press, who were
fascinated by the sight of the harnessed workers rappelling from bubble to bubble, scrubbing the four thousand "pillows," as if this were a
performance that had been planned to further integrate architecture
into the spectacle of the Olympics.

If Lever House demonstrated a particular way of life and the cleanliness of the company's products, the Water Cube demonstrates the
government's ability to clean its polluted city and amass workers for
a demonstration that is both a performance and a spectacle of man
dominating nature.

GEKKO Façade and Clean Ant: Window-Washing Robots, 2009

GEKKO Façade and Clean Ant are two of the latest developments in window-washing robots on the market, introduced by the Swiss company Serbot AG in 2009. The robots can be permanently installed to roam around the façade at set intervals. According to Serbot, they clean windows at a faster pace than people do and can be fully automated or, if necessary, operated over radio control.[19] They attach to the façade with rotating vacuum feet, and they can move in all directions. The Clean Ant has the additional capability of being able to work across curved surfaces because of its pivoting legs. While the robots can be implemented on existing buildings, they perform best when they are integrated at the design and planning stage. The robots are indicative of the changing responsibilities of architect and developer, which increasingly include the development of new maintenance systems.

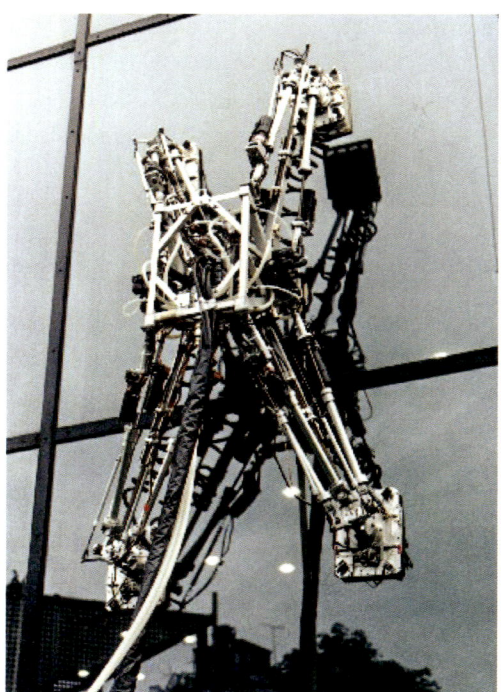

4.18
Ninja. © Advanced Robotic Vehicles.

5
POST-OCCUPANCY AND ALTERNATE ARCHITECTURAL FUTURES

Post-occupancy describes the period of time after a building is finished, when inhabitants have begun to use it. The term prioritizes the life of the building over its design or its form, playing off the professional definition of *occupancy* that describes the number of building users for an occupancy type (assembly, office, residential, and so on). Post-occupancy offers a means to consider prolonging the relationship between building and architect. If the responsibility of the architect were extended, how would design practice and buildings change?

5.1

Sarah Morris, *AM/PM*, 1999, production
still from the film. Photc credit:
Andrea Stappert.

AM/PM, Sarah Morris, 1999

The film *AM/PM*, by the artist, painter, and filmmaker Sarah Morris, is a study in a kind of solitary maintenance—the lone figure washing each pane of glass and spandrel panel. In the case of Las Vegas, mainte-nance work seems especially lonely. The solitary figure of the service worker is the focus of this video still. Morris states that she wanted to capture "the other side of the tourism industry."[1] Her films often bring together things in stark opposition or contrast to each other: the luxurious with the mundane. *AM/PM* does this by capturing the lone window washer, suspended in a bosun's chair in front of an intensely reflective golden tinted-glass façade. This type of device replaces the belt-and-hook method of earlier years, but is perhaps no safer. Remi-niscent of Karsten Harries's description and framing of the terror of time, Morris captures this effect by zooming in on a decadent building being cleaned in the cheapest way possible. The urban environment is reflected in the building at a safe distance from the camera, but not a comfortable one. In her later film, *Beijing*, the "colourless" images seem to reference both Roland Barthes's description of his first trip to China and the country's well-known environmental problems and heavily polluted air.[2] Morris's views of cities have an intense lushness of effect.

Endurance

So far we have discussed several historical developments in the domestication of upkeep. One has to do with the production of maintenance, another with the class who maintains; endurance has to do with the consumption of buildings that makes maintenance so necessary.

When consumption is private, maintenance must also be individualized. Maintenance is considered a responsibility of home ownership, and entails personal expenditure. The individualization of consumption and the collectivization of design have further exacerbated the divide that maintenance must bridge. This divide puts maintenance workers and machines in the contradictory position of having to care for complex and specialized buildings that are individually owned.

Although maintenance tasks often require the exchange of capital with a specialist (an electrician, a plumber, a contractor), their segregation puts the burden of maintenance on an individual, and thus becomes a singular desire. The maintenance worker's desire can be made collective only by converting it into the homogeneous medium of capital—hardly an effective way to redistribute desire.

These conditions lead us to an understanding of maintenance as a practice necessitated by the limitations of architecture, but also as a product of history and its continuous formal interpretation. Dirt and dust need to be cleaned off surfaces, and waste needs to be removed. Much of the history of maintenance points to its privatization as a practice, and as such the categories of domestic upkeep are well defined and have become more organized through technologies such as self-cleaning glass, rendering household upkeep more aligned to "managed" maintenance.

However, domestic maintenance has seen great transformations in the modern age. Suburbanization and the increased role of private property have led to stronger divisions between public and private spheres. Even something like the development of plumbing in the eighteenth and nineteenth centuries caused the emerging industries of hygiene and waste treatment to become privatized. In that regard, reaching to the domestic realm, maintaining personal hygiene, along with living in a clean house, became inseparable with respect to being perceived as healthy. This thinking about maintenance and upkeep of the built environment collapsed across a variety of building types, from the sanatorium and the clinic to the modern house, and was even adopted in the artist's studio. The use of white walls became the symbol or representation of cleanliness as essential to preserving both personal and societal health. Modern architecture was more than just "simply white," but rendering it as such helped to reinforce the idea that it was eternally new, and stayed that way without any effort.[3]

The relative ease with which we categorize domestic cleanliness and the ubiquity of these practices are the result of what the phenomenologist Maurice Merleau-Ponty has called "sedimentation," defined as "an attitude towards the world [that], when it has received frequent confirmation, acquires a favored status for us."[4] Sedimentation happens both collectively and personally through culture, habit, and, in particular, language. Maintenance is perhaps now finally receiving such a framing through contemporary art projects and an increasing number of larger architectural works that require continual cleaning.

Loomis House, William Lescaze, 1938

Completed in 1938, the Loomis Glass House in Tuxedo Park, New York, represents a first in the United States by using glass to insulate its exterior walls. Conceived as a "house within a house," the interior living space was enveloped by a double-glazed "passage" that buffered it from the elements in an attempt to re-create the semitropical climate of Hilton Head Island, South Carolina, within.[5] The owner, Alfred Lee Loomis, was a prominent American financier, attorney, and amateur scientist who owned nearly all of Hilton Head Island, where he vacationed; now he wanted to simulate its climate up north in order to enjoy it year round. Known for his novel inventions and experimental scientific research projects—from a study of brain waves and their intersection with epilepsy that led to the redesign of the EEG machine, to research with time and ultrasound—Loomis was a founding member of MIT's "Rad Lab," a top-secret wartime laboratory, and an original board member of RAND Corporation.[6] His interest in environmental control led to the design of the Glass House, where he combined solar principles popular in the early 1930s with the most advanced and modernistic heating, cooling, and lighting systems.[7]

First, Loomis designed and built a sun machine that tracked the sun across the wooded site to determine the optimal location for the house, based on solar principles. He was then introduced to the Swiss architect William E. Lescaze by his longtime science collaborator, Garrett Hobart IV, for whom Lescaze had designed an all-concrete house in Tuxedo Park in 1937. Lescaze, along with George Howe, had already applied "air-pressure and air-conditioning" systems at the PSFS Building in Philadelphia (1932), but their application on the scale of the house would not become widespread until after World War II. Using these systems in a home, according to Lescaze, was a result of Loomis's scientific desire "to experiment with a novel system of heating and airconditions" outside of the laboratory in "ordinary living conditions," and in doing so, over a longer period of time, to "investigate the effects of living in such an atmosphere."[8] To maintain an artificial climate, the house was built with a raised floor, double-shell ceiling, and the double-glazed passage around its perimeter to encase the building in a layer of warm air.[9] Put to the test, however, the experimental solar strategy of the "passage," which had been built without operable windows, significantly strained the custom-built, room-sized air conditioner to the point of breakdown.

Unité d'Habitation in Berlin, Le Corbusier, 1957

At Le Corbusier's Unité in Berlin, the *Strasse* or street inserts itself inside the building, creating a skip-stop section and an impressively wide corridor at its heart. Along with the idea of bringing the street inside, however, came another dialogue about how to maintain that street. Figures 5.2 to 5.4 show how Le Corbusier uses paint to color code each floor. The sizes of doors differ between the main entrance door, the apartment door, the small service window, and the service closet doors to shafts beyond. The intention to create a physical world within the building can be achieved only by thinking through the problem of maintenance, and here Le Corbusier—as in the Cité de Refuge—is thinking about the organization of every aspect of his work before it is constructed.

5.2–5.4
Le Corbusier, Unité d'Habitation,
Berlin, 1957. Photographs by
the author.

5.5
Louis Kahn, Yale Center for British Art,
1974, steel and glass detail. Photograph
by the author.

Yale Center for British Art, Louis Kahn, 1974

This frontal elevation of Louis Kahn's Yale Center for British Art, completed after his death in 1974, shows a façade that is complete, solid, and maintenance-free. Looking like stained concrete or stone, as do so many of Kahn's buildings, this face of the building is actually made up of prefinished steel panels. Built just after the urban renewal period of the late 1960s, the uniformly gray British Art Center (BAC) projects a kind of uneasiness in the context of Yale University and the city of New Haven, with its slight distortions and exposed seams. In 2010 the city demolished the full-block Coliseum building by Dinkeloo and Roche in an effort to remove some of the failed urban renewal projects built at the time of the BAC. While the BAC was not such a project, it is important to note the context of its development, since it is being restored while projects built at the same time have been removed from the city's fabric. In many ways the particular aesthetics of the building are a result of the political, economic, and cultural underpinnings of New Haven, but they also pay homage to the legacy of Kahn's work, as much of the building had to be imagined after his death. Its largely opaque exterior belies an extraordinary inner world, with a light-filled grand hall and an atmosphere of privilege and excellence. To restore the building, a plan was drawn up, entitled "Louis I. Kahn and the Yale Center for British Art: A Conservation Plan," which has been touted as the first of its kind in the United States, as it calls for some parts of the building to be preserved and maintained while other elements will be more freely changed.[10]

5.6–5.7

SANAA, Toledo Glass Pavilion, 2006.
Courtesy of SANAA.

Toledo Museum of Art Glass Pavilion, SANAA, 2006

SANAA's Glass Pavilion at the Toledo Museum of Art in Ohio houses the museum's renowned glass collection, a glass-making workshop, and temporary exhibition galleries. The building is a design object in its own right, an impressive feat of glass and structural design. Because the glass is not load-bearing, the Pavilion has a series of slender steel interior supports and a roof that houses the majority of its electrical and mechanical systems.[11] The glass wall works like an insulated glazing unit (IGU), with a vacuum-filled cavity that minimizes heat transfer. The building's use of radiant heating in the floor and ceiling also mitigates the temperature differential between inside and out.[12]

The reappearance in contemporary practice of the double-glazed façade is a legacy of early modernism's environmental control projects. The double-glazed wrapper has increasingly been implemented to create efficacy in the performance of fully glazed buildings. Its adoption at the Toledo Glass Pavilion produced an architecture concerned with microclimates.

However, the vast amount of glass in the Pavilion—some 360 panels measuring eight by thirteen and a half feet—is hardly maintenance-free. The task of maintaining the Pavilion's sense of transparency falls to its janitorial staff. The doors, in particular, must be washed several times a day using a fairly standard squeegee method. According to one museum employee, there are sometimes even face prints on the glass.[13]

Dutch Embassy in Berlin, Rem Koolhaas/OMA, 2004

The site for Koolhaas/OMA's Dutch Embassy in Berlin is located on a typical Berlin courtyard block. Koolhaas kept the original block blown open to preserve the city's memory of war and to acknowledge, reflect, and embody the openness of Dutch society. The two volumes of the building are separated by a gap but woven together through a ramp, stairs, and bridges. The building "twists and turns in upon itself" and also uses its own infrastructure for cleaning. Mechanical ducting and air flow are included as part of the "trajectory."[14] The glass and aluminum finishes move toward a finer and smoother palette of materials than were used in previous projects, and aesthetically suggest a new direction, leaving behind the roughness of OMA's 1992 Rotterdam Kunsthal. It is not that the work is necessarily interested in a primary reading of the building as remaining eternally new, but as transparent and permeable. Even the overall form is indebted to a rethinking of building in the city, and the creation of an organized formal building that reflects Berlin's history more than the structure itself. Creating two volumes separated by exterior space produces two kinds of maintenance space. The thin, perforated-metal-clad bar behind the main cube of the embassy holds five apartments that require a particular kind of upkeep; in the transparent and open street volume, maintenance is undertaken from within—interior lights of glass swing open to be cleaned from the inside. The inside is always renewed and kept clean, seemingly fixed, while the outside is never complete because the block remains open.

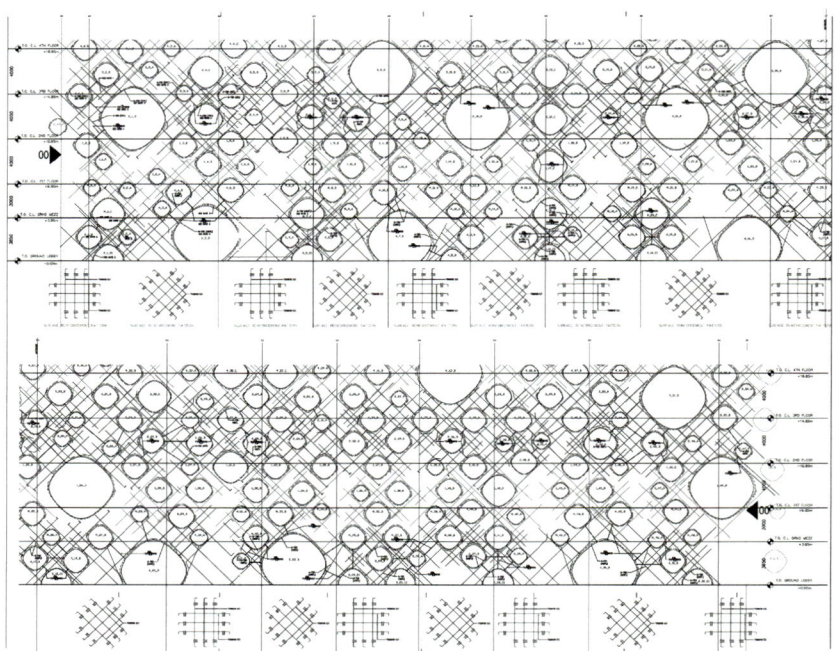

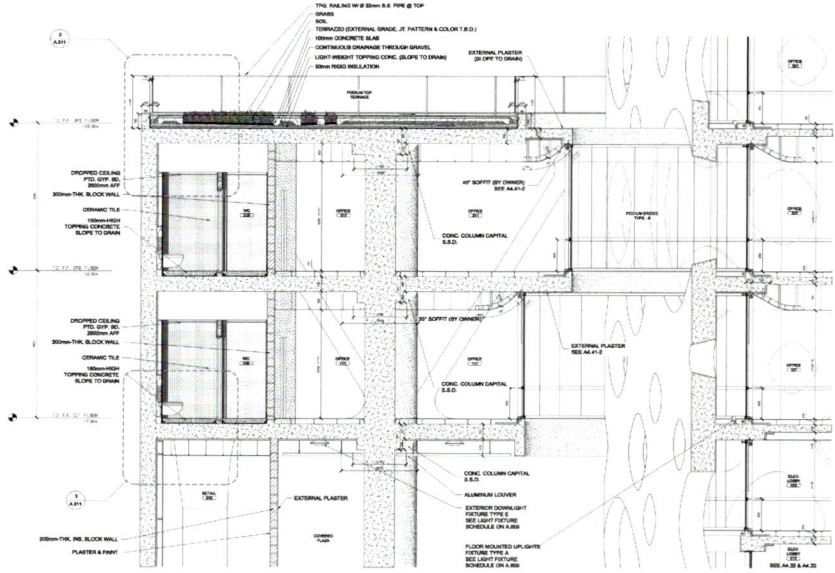

5.11 (top)

Reiser + Umemoto, O-14, 2010, unrolled elevation. Courtesy of Reiser + Umemoto.

5.12 (bottom)

Reiser + Umemoto, O-14, 2010, detail section. Courtesy of Reiser + Umemoto.

O-14, Reiser + Umemoto, 2010

In the age of self-cleaning buildings, there remains a desire for whiteness and pureness. O-14, the commercial office tower designed by architects Reiser + Umemoto for Dubai's Business Bay, epitomizes this trend. The finished 22-story office building, once painted white, bears an uncanny resemblance to its initial rendering, a relationship that is ever in flux in the harsh, arid climate of Dubai.[15]

The "maintenance-free" or "self-cleaning" qualities of buildings cannot be considered separately from their materials. O-14's porous concrete exoskeleton, subject to wind and desert sands, continuously weeps dust and other air pollutants, subtly changing color and appearance over time.[16] Jesse Reiser writes: "The tower's concrete shell not only is the structure of the building but also creates a lace-like façade open to light, air, and views."[17] The perforated concrete shell regulates light, views, and structural requirements. Hot air circulates upward to cool the building, thanks to the one-meter gap that separates the shell and the glass window walls. This gap also enables the windows to be easily and safely washed.[18]

The fascination with self-cleaning, once a domestic dream in Fuller's Dymaxion House, has now been adopted in the public realm, leading to unprecedented material combinations and structural manifestations. If architecture represents forms of endurance, its material specificity underscores an overall relationship to social and economic structures. The Pittsburgh headquarters of Alcoa, U.S. Steel, and PPG were urban projections of contemporary achievements, shifting from past staid principles to new proprietary ideas about the future of building, and how these ideas ought to be considered in the context of the energy of the city. The last decade has shown a shift toward the necessity for architecture to be social and visionary, and not tied to any corporation— so that the building is viewed not as self-promotion by the business within it, but as a sign that architecture's relevancy and agency are increasing.

I Feel Cold Today, Patrick Bernatchez, 2007

Shelter promises protection from time's terror.
Karsten Harries, "Building and the Terror of Time"[19]

Architecture is one of the basic strategies that all cultures use
to mediate between the helpless individual and the power
of nature's absolutely unbearable laws. As well as protecting
us physically, man-made structures attempt to humanize
nature by giving the illusion that nature cares about us,
that nature has a human face. Architecture makes a human order—
an illusion, but a great one—in the heart of nature's world.
Vincent Scully, *The Architecture of Community*[20]

Architectural images are above all representations of a promised future, and maintenance mediates between architecture's future presence and its obsolescence. Shelter, promising protection from the "terror of time," succumbs as the natural world invades it.[21] This invasion of the natural is beautifully depicted in the 2007 film *I Feel Cold Today* by Montreal filmmaker Patrick Bernatchez.[22]

In an ethereal and otherworldly effect, the film presents the stark interiors of a generic office building, seemingly built in the 1960s and never updated. As a result, its interiors seem trapped in a moment that remains eternally present.[23] They look deserted, with a feeling of abrupt abandonment, as if everything has been emptied out only to decay and be filled back in. Suddenly the blinds in the conference room begin moving, as if being pushed aside by the internal breezes of a fan. The movement of the blinds becomes stronger and more intense within minutes, suggesting that the force is not human or mechanical, but wild and natural, and it continues to amplify with the intensity of a growing storm. Within moments the wind carries snow flurries into the frame of the scene. Snow begins to float through the space, eventually accumulating on the office floor in mounds, creating a soft undulating interior that covers the terrain of what were once hard edges of tables, desks, and cabinetry.

The color of the light created by the snow, a grayish white, is a stark contrast to more conventional and familiar fluorescent office lighting.

Rather than appearing otherworldly or ethereal, the new interior terrain within the office floor plate suggests a future post-apocalyptic setting. *I Feel Cold Today* speaks to the loss of momentum in Montreal at the end of the 1960s and the decline of its urbanity in a post-Expo landscape. It also speaks more broadly to the general failure of the modern movement.

Bernatchez's film also emphasizes the temporal transformation of space. A once animated office devoid of life and replaced with wild nature is a significant commentary on place and material. It speaks to the uneven development of Montreal as a city of projects, and to the failure of the glass tower typology that depends on artificial systems of heating, cooling, and lighting.

I Feel Cold Today also presents an environment distorted by abandonment. The technology and construction of the tower produce an inert object. The failure of the tower's glass curtain wall—the presumed cause of the snow's infiltration—destabilizes the mass of the building and its environmentally controlled workspace. Heating and air-conditioning are replaced by wind, chill, and snow. The snow's rapid accumulation suggests that the building has been vacant for some time, with a tie and a bottle left behind as relics of a previous culture. It is like walking in a dream. These scenes of the outmoded building awaiting rehabilitation or demolition depict both possible futures in the history of architecture and capitalism.

There is a kind of intimacy in seeing these forlorn office spaces being overwhelmed by nature, breaking from the real experience of this place and the projection it casts on its past memories. Within this exaggerated environment, no subject ever appears. The film captures a moment in the continuum of the life of the building. The mundane office eventually becomes a forlorn office, then a wasteland. Its wondrous natural setting presents an irrational and unserendipitous view of the archetypal office building. *I Feel Cold Today* renders an uncanny and unexpected view of the future.

With its focus on environment, formalism, and space, the film fulfills the artist's predilection for abrupt contrasts between inert places and violent urban or environmental acts—which are typically shown

only from the exterior. If we think of events like the Pruitt-Igoe housing demolition and the collapse of the World Trade Center towers on 9/11, rarely are we given a glimpse of internal decay. It can be argued that the filmmaker plays provocateur and examines modernism's stark future, in which dystopia and primitivism take hold. The echoing walk through the vacant corporate office further attenuates the distance between present, past, and future. Although saying that our future is laid out in a few moments within a rather languishing film may seem to give the film too much credit, its significance lies in the imagery it provokes.

The endurance of architecture's image persists as a twofold problem. The first problem is the profusion of platforms for architectural representation today: the Internet, films, books, and journals. The second problem is that the systems within actual buildings are expected to last a significant amount of time. Modernism applied the latest industrialized parts and systems to architecture to help promote new ways of living, especially healthy living, but those technologies have not all endured. Architects today share those same objectives: to make buildings perform better, and be more cost- and energy-efficient, in order to contribute to a better lifestyle.

The maintenance of architectural surfaces remains extremely important, as illustrated by the significant number of projects with glass and white surfaces explored in this book. However, there are two camps: one in favor of all glass, total transparency; another that aspires to all-white and opaque. If anything, maintenance does not disappear with the advent of technology; instead it becomes increasingly necessary. As mechanized solutions for cleaning and maintenance are introduced, the human figure may disappear for a time, but our need for maintenance cannot be completely eliminated. Inevitably there will be breakdowns, glitches, failures, and unexpected consequences. Architecture's value is based as much on its contingencies as on its aesthetics and form. If architecture is the most technological of the arts, as a practice it seems to be increasingly reliant upon specialists and professionals rather than artists to ensure its enduring image. If we return to the Smithsons' *Heroic Period* prediction for the future, we would now be recording "built-places," air views, sequential photographs, and systemic explanations. Maintenance is a key part of this form of visualization of either buildings or built places. In perpetuating the illusion of newness, modernism created a myth about architecture's very being. These works of art, put together here for the first time in a series, pose a question about the problems of realism and the myth of modernism, a myth of the seemingly real and certainly the previously unseen.[24]

Notes

INTRODUCTION

1. Interview with Donald Wall (1975), Canadian Centre for Architecture Archives.
2. Hilary Sample, "Maintenance Architecture," *Praxis*, no. 6 (2004), 114–121.
3. Ibid.
4. Hannah Arendt, *The Human Condition* (Chicago: University of Chicago Press, 1998), 2nd edn.
5. Pier Vittorio Aureli, conference introduction, "Architecture and Labor," a symposium organized by Aureli and the PhD program "City/Architecture," Architectural Association, London, November 13, 2015, <http://www.aaschool. ac.uk/VIDEO/lecture.php?ID=3256> (accessed March 1, 2015); Arendt, *The Human Condition*.
6. Martin Heidegger, "The Question Concerning Technology," in *Basic Writings*, ed. David Farrell Krell (San Francisco: Harper, 1993), 141.
7. Alison Smithson and Peter Smithson, "Prelude" to *The Heroic Period of Modern Architecture* (New York: Rizzoli, 1981), 5. The Smithsons wrote the "Prelude" in 1965, but their book was not published until 1981.
8. Heidegger, "The Question Concerning Technology," 147.
9. Ibid., 146.
10. Ibid., 147.
11. Ibid., 311.
12. David Gissen, *Manhattan Atmospheres: Architecture, the Interior Environment, and Urban Crisis* (Minneapolis and London: University of Minnesota Press, 2014), 18–19.
13. Nelson Goodman, *Ways of Worldmaking* (Indianapolis: Hackett Publishing, 1978), 70.
14. Rem Koolhaas, "Cronocaos," *Log*, no. 21 (Winter 2011), 119.
15. Esther da Costa Meyer, review of *Cronocaos*, *Journal of the Society of Architectural Historians* 71, no. 2 (June 2012), 248–249. Meyer notes that "*Cronocaos* also perpetuates stereotypes concerning gender."
16. See Rem Koolhaas with Jorge Pailos-Otero, *Preservation Is Overtaking Us* (New York: GSAPP Books, 2014).
17. Rem Koolhaas, "Preface," in AMO/Rem Koolhaas, eds., *Domus d'Autore, Post-Occupancy* (Domus, 2006).
18. Karsten Harries, *The Ethical Function of Architecture* (Cambridge, MA: MIT Press, 1998), 255.

19. Alice T. Friedman, *Women and the Making of the Modern House: A Social and Architectural History* (New Haven: Yale University Press, 2006), 132–133.

20. Jacques Derrida, *Archive Fever*, trans. Eric Prenowitz (Chicago: University of Chicago Press, 1995), 78.

21. Ibid.

22. Harries, *The Ethical Function of Architecture*, 264.

23. Ibid., 261.

24. Ibid., 256.

25. Ibid., 119.

26. Smithson and Smithson, *The Heroic Period of Modern Architecture*, 5.

27. Ibid.

CHAPTER 1

1. Hilary Sample, "Maintenance Architecture," *Praxis*, no. 6 (2004), 114–121.

2. Rem Koolhaas, *Delirious New York* (New York: Monacelli Press, 1994), 230.

3. Ibid.

4. Ibid., 178.

5. Hilary Sample, "Towers, Maintenance, and the Desire for Effortless Performance," in Joshua Bolchover and Jonathan D. Solomon, eds., *Sustain and Develop*, 306090 Books, no. 13 (New York: Princeton Architectural Press, 2010), 80–84.

6. Vanessa van Dam, in discussion with the author, February 2009.

7. For more on Lever House, see below in this chapter.

8. Martin Heidegger, "The Question Concerning Technology," in *Basic Writings*, ed. David Farrell Krell (San Francisco: Harper, 1993), 147.

9. "Window Washers Meet by Radio," *Popular Science* (July 1937), 29.

10. See the section on the squeegee in chapter 4.

11. Reyner Banham, *The Architecture of the Well-Tempered Environment*, 2nd ed. (Chicago: University of Chicago Press, 1984), 227.

12. Reinhold Martin, *The Organizational Complex: Architecture, Media, and Corporate Space* (Cambridge, MA: MIT Press, 2003), 102.

13. Katy Siegel, "Jennifer Bolande: Appliance House," *Artforum* (January 2000), 88–89.

14. Carsten Krohn, *Mies van der Rohe: The Built Work* (Basel: Birkhäuser, 2014), 158.

15. Ibid., 294.

16. Reyner Banham, "The Glass Paradise," in *A Critic Writes* (Berkeley: University of California Press, 1996), 36.

17. Martin, *The Organizational Complex*, 102.

18. "Aluminum Skyscraper," *Popular Mechanics* (December 1953), 87.

19. David Bear, "The Next Page: High Point Pittsburgh's Lofty Ambition," *Pittsburgh Post-Gazette*, March 10, 2013.

20. "About PPG Place," *PPG Place*, <http://www.ppgplace.com/about/> (accessed August 29, 2015).

21. Mark Wigley, *White Walls, Designer Dresses: The Fashioning of Modern Architecture* (Cambridge, MA: MIT Press, 2001).

22. Thomas C. Jester, "Aluminum Finishes in Postwar Architecture," special issue, *APT Bulletin* 46, no. 1 (2015), 43.

23. Hilary Sample, "Natalie de Blois," in Eva Franch i Gilabert et al., eds., *OfficeUS Agenda* (New York: Storefront for Art and Architecture, 2014), 65–80.

24. Robert Gutman, "The Organizational Client," in *Architectural Practice: A Critical View* (New York: Princeton Architectural Press, 1988), 50–60.

25. John Vinocur, "Pei's Pyramid Design for the Louvre Sparks Debate in Paris," *New York Times*, February 27, 1984, <http://www.nytimes.com/1984/02/27/arts/pei-s-pyramid-design-for-the-louvre-sparks-debate-in-paris.html> (accessed August 29, 2015).

CHAPTER 2

1. Mierle Laderman Ukeles, "Manifesto for Maintenance Art 1969! Proposal for an Exhibition 'CARE'," 1. Copyright Mierle Laderman.

2. Sigmund Freud, *Beyond the Pleasure Principle and Other Writings* (New York: Penguin Adult, 2003).

3. Tom Finkelpearl, "Mierle Ukeles on Maintenance and Sanitation Art," in *Dialogues in Public Art* (Cambridge, MA: MIT Press, 2000), 303.

4. Ibid.

5. Ibid.

6. Ibid.

7. Italo Calvino, *Invisible Cities* (New York: Houghton Mifflin Harcourt, 2013), 114.

8. Susan Sontag, *Styles of Radical Will* (New York: Picador, 1969), 31.

9. Ibid., 46.

10. Sylvia Lavin, at the University of Michigan, Practice Session #1, November 16, 2015.

11. Michael Bell, introduction to Michael Bell and Jeannie Kim, eds., *Engineered Transparency: The Technical, Visual, and Spatial Effects of Glass* (New York: Princeton Architectural Press, 2008), 15.

12. Reyner Banham, *The Architecture of the Well-Tempered Environment*, 2nd ed. (Chicago: University of Chicago Press, 1998), 145.

13. Joan Ockman, "A Crystal World: Between Reason and Spectacle," in Bell and Kim, eds., *Engineered Transparency*, 45, 47.

14. Bell, introduction to Bell and Kim, eds., *Engineered Transparency*, 15.

15. Le Corbusier, *When the Cathedrals Were White* (New York: Reynal & Hitchcock, 1947).

16. Andy Warhol, *The Philosophy of Andy Warhol (From A to B and Back Again)* (New York: Harcourt Brace Jovanovich, 1975), 159.

17. "Who Were the 'White Wings'?," *New York Historical Society and Library*, <http://www.nyhistory.org/community/white-wings> (accessed August 29, 2015).

18. Catherine de Smet and John Cullars, "About One Striped Rectangle: Jean Widmer and the Centre Pompidou Logo," *Design Issues* 26, no. 1 (Winter 2010), 67–81.

19. Bettina Vismann and Jürgen Mayer H., "The Perspiration Affair, or the New National Gallery between Cold Fronts," *Grey Room* 09 (Fall 2002), 89.

20. Martin Heidegger, "The Question Concerning Technology," in *Basic Writings*, ed. David Farrell Krell (San Francisco: Harper, 1993), 337.

21. Jacques Lacan, "Subversion of the Subject and the Dialectic of Desire in the Freudian Unconscious," in *Écrits: A Selection*, trans. Alan Sheridan (London: Routledge 1977), 301.

22. Alice T. Friedman, "People Who Live in Glass Houses: Edith Farnsworth, Ludwig Mies van der Rohe, and Philip Johnson," in *Women and the Making of the Modern House: A Social and Architectural History* (New Haven: Yale University Press, 2006), 129.

23. Yevgeny Zamyatin, *We*, trans. Clarence Brown (New York: Penguin Books, 1993).

24. Joan Ockman, "Review: Housing Projects, *Women and the Making of the Modern House: A Social and Architectural History*, by Alice T. Friedman," *Women's Review of Books* 16, no. 2 (November 1998), 22–23.

25. Pamela Allara, "Iñigo Manglano-Ovalle: Pie in the Sky," *Art New England* (June/July 2002).

CHAPTER 3

1. Ila Bêka and Louise Lemoine, *Diary/Journal* (Paris: Bêka & Partners, 2013).

2. Rem Koolhaas, interview by Ila Bêka and Louise Lemoine, *Koolhaas Houselife*, DVD, directed by Ila Bêka and Louise Lemoine (Paris: Bêka Films, 2008).

3. Ibid.

4. Ibid.

5. For essential writing on this subject, see Elaine Scarry, *The Body in Pain: The Making and Unmaking of the World* (New York: Oxford University Press, 1985).

6. For example, Le Corbusier called architecture a "pure creation of the mind" dependent upon emotions and relations, which stands in juxtaposition to mere construction. See *Toward an Architecture*, trans. John Goodman (Los Angeles: Getty, 2007), 97, 231–251.

7. Rolf Lauter, "Interiors: Humans and Their Lifeworld," in *Jeff Wall, Figures and Places: Selected Works from 1978 to 2000*, ed. Rolf Lauter (London: Prestel, 2001), 54–55.

8. Martin Heidegger, "The Question Concerning Technology," in *Basic Writings*, ed. David Farrell Krell (San Francisco: Harper, 1993), 319.

9. Donald Wall, "Gordon Matta-Clark's Building Dissections," *Arts Magazine* (March 1976), 74–79.

10. Carel Blotkamp and Sjoukje van der Meulen, *New Dutch Sculptors: Job Koelewijn* (Rijssen, Netherlands: New Sculpture Museum Foundation, 1999), 12.

11. Adam Szymczyk, "Job Koelewijn Fail Better," in *Post Nature: Nine Dutch Artists; Biennale di Venezia* (Rotterdam: NAi Publishers, 2001), 28.

12. Blotkamp and van der Meulen, *New Dutch Sculptors*, 13.

13. Job Koelewijn, *Cleaning the Rietveld Pavilion*, self-published, limited edition book, 1992, 8. A special thanks to Bas Peters for the translation.

14. Ibid., 21.

15. Rietveld designed other pavilions—De Zonnehof (1959) in Amersfoort, the Netherlands; the Sonsbeek Pavilion (1955) now located in the sculpture garden of the Kröller-Müller Museum in Otterlo, the Netherlands; and the Dutch Pavilion (1953) for the Venice Biennale in Venice, Italy.

16. Gerrit Th. Rietveld, *The Complete Works*, ed. Marijke Kuper and Ida van Zijl (Utrecht: Centraal Museum Utrecht, 1992), 17.

17. History of Gerrit Rietveld Academie, *Gerrit Rietveld Academie*, <http://www.gerritrietveldacademie.nl/en/history> (accessed February 26, 2015).

18. Luca Cerizza, *Job Koelewijn: History Future*, Galerie Fons Welters (November 2003), 49.

19. Ibid., 53.

20. Ibid., 49.

21. Jorge Otero-Pailos, *Jorge Otero-Pailos: The Ethics of Dust* (Cologne: Walther König, 2009), 9.

22. Ibid., 21.

23. See <http://www.new-territories.com/roche2002bis.htm>.

24. Ibid.

25. Rotor, *How Things Stand* (Brussels: Éditions de la Communauté française Wallonie-Bruxelles, 2010), 56–57.

26. This statement by Rotor recalls one of Bernard Tschumi's "Advertisements for Architecture" that depicts the Villa Savoye in 1965 with the caption: "The most architectural thing about this building is the state of decay in which it is." Tschumi is less interested in the humanizing effects of use on a building than he is in the political power it has the potential to generate: "Architecture only survives where it negates the form that society expects of it. Where it negates itself by transgressing the limits that history has set for it." It is only when a project loses its allure as a perfect object and undergoes the morphosis wrought by human habitation, natural elements, and time that it takes on transcendent qualities.

185

3. Federico Neder, *Fuller Houses: R. Buckminster Fuller's Dymaxion Dwellings and Other Domestic Adventures,* trans. Elsa Lam (Baden: Lars Müller Publishers, 2008), 38, 127.

4. Mark Wigley, foreword to Neder, *Fuller Houses,* 14.

5. Buckminster Fuller, quoted in Reyner Banham, *Theory and Design in the First Machine Age* (London: Architectural Press, 1961), 325–326.

6. Beatriz Colomina, "Unbreathed Air 1956," *Grey Room* 15 (Spring 2004), 50.

7. Ibid.

8. Ibid., 33.

9. Jonathan Sterne, "Space within Space: Artificial Reverb and the Detachable Echo," *Grey Room* 60 (Summer 2015).

10. Kim Boatman, "World Would Have Looked Duller without Squeegee Company," *Seattle Times*, April 13, 2004, <http://old.seattletimes.com/html/businesstechnology/2001901752_squeegee07.html> (accessed August 29, 2015).

11. Ibid.

12. "History," *Ettore*, <http://www.ettore.com/professionals/about-us/history/> (accessed August 29, 2015).

13. A New York City socialite of German descent, Anna Dormitzer became one of the leading patent holders in the United States in the late 1800s, and part of a small group of women who experimented with technological gadgets for the home. See Autumn Stanley, *Mothers and Daughters of Invention: Notes for a Revised History of Technology* (New Brunswick: Rutgers University Press, 1993), 315.

14. The Step-Chair included metal rods, chains, and wires to hold the actual cleaning articles, and could be folded up for storage. For detailed drawings, see Anna Dormitzer, Improvement in Window-Cleaning Step-Chairs, US Patent 206,936, filed April 16, 1878, issued August 13, 1878.

15. See William H. Clarke, Extensible Window-Washing Device, US Patent 825,879, filed February 12, 1906, issued July 10, 1906; Clinton C. De Witt, Hydropneumatic Window-Cleaning Apparatus, US Patent 1,114,592, filed February 26, 1914, issued October 20, 1914.

16. "Volume-Added Flat-Glass Products for the Building Transportation Markets, Part 2," *American Ceramic Society Bulletin* 84, no. 4 (April 2005), 34–40.

17. "How It Works," *Pilkington*, <http://www.pilkington.com/products/bp/bybenefit/selfcleaning/how+it+works.htm> (accessed August 17, 2015).

18. Joseph A. Amato, *Dust: A History of the Small and the Invisible* (Berkeley: University of California Press, 2000), 80.

19. "GEKKO Façade," *Serbot Swiss Innovations*, <http://www.serbot.ch/en/products/facade-cleaning/gekko-facade> (accessed August 29, 2015).

CHAPTER 5

1. *Sarah Morris*, exh. cat. (Zurich: Sarah Morris & Kunsthalle, 2000), 56.

2. Johanna Burton, "Just Breathe: Sarah Morris's Beijing," in *Sarah Morris: Lesser Panda* (London: White Cube, 2008), 11–13.

3. Mark Wigley, *White Walls, Designer Dresses: The Fashioning of Modern Architecture* (Cambridge, MA: MIT Press, 1995), xv.

4. Maurice Merleau-Ponty, *Phenomenology of Perception*, trans. Colin Smith (New York: Humanities Press, 1962), 441–442.

5. Tuxedo Park was Loomis's permanent residence between 1926 and 1950. Jennet Conant, *Tuxedo Park: A Wall Street Tycoon and the Secret Palace of Science that Changed the Course of World War II* (New York: Simon and Schuster, 2003), 97–99; Luis W. Alvarez, "Alfred Lee Loomis—Last Great Amateur of Science," *Physics Today* 36, no. 1 (January 1983), 25–34.

6. For more information on Loomis, see Conant, *Tuxedo Park*, 112; Warren P. Mason, "Sonics and Ultrasonics: Early History and Applications," *IEEE Transactions on Sonics and Ultrasonics* 23, no. 4 (July 1976), 226; "Radar Secrets," *Science News-Letter* 48, no. 8 (August 1945), 115–116.

7. Daniel Barber, "The Modern Solar House: Architecture, Energy, and the Emergence of Environmentalism, 1938–1959," PhD diss., Columbia University, 2010.

8. Conant, *Tuxedo Park*, 188–189.

9. The technical kit of parts used to construct the house included prefabricated steel columns, metal decking, an air-conditioning unit, and metal ducts. All noisy and vibrating mechanical devices were wrapped in insulation, every surface of the mechanical room was lined with a four-inch layer of cork, and acoustical tiles lined the conservatory's ceiling, creating an atmosphere so silent that not even raindrops could be heard hitting the glass skylights.

10. "The Louis I. Kahn Building," *The Yale Center for British Art*, <http://britishart.yale.edu/architecture> (accessed December 6, 2015).

11. "Glass Pavilion Architecture," *Toledo Museum of Art*, <www.toledomuseum.org/glass-pavilion/architecture> (accessed August 31, 2015).

12. Michael Bell and Jeannie Kim, eds., *Engineered Transparency: The Technical, Visual, and Spatial Effects of Glass* (New York: Princeton Architectural Press, 2009), 119.

13. "Glass Pavilion Window Washing," *The Blade*, January 30, 2012, <www.toledoblade.com/local/2012/01/30/Glass-Pavilion-window-washing.html> (accessed August 29, 2015).

14. François Chaslin, *The Dutch Embassy in Berlin by OMA/Rem Koolhaas* (Rotterdam: NAi Publishers, 2004).

15. Jesse Reiser, "O-14—Dubai, UAE," lecture, Museum of Modern Art, New York, September 21, 2013.

16. Ibid.

17. "O-14," RUR Architecture, PC, <http://www.reiser-umemoto.com/> (accessed August 29, 2015).

18. Reiser + Umemoto, *O-14: Projection and Reception*, ed. Brett Steele (London: AA Publications, 2012), 111.

19. Karsten Harries, "Building and the Terror of Time," *Perspecta*, no. 19 (1982), 59.

20. Vincent Scully, *The Architecture of Community* (Ann Arbor: University of Michigan, 1996), 8.

21. Harries, "Building and the Terror of Time," 59.
22. Patrick Bernatchez, *I Feel Cold Today*, 2007, filmstrip.
23. Ibid.
24. Roland Barthes, *S/Z*, cited in Rosalind E. Krauss, *The Originality of the Avant-Garde and Other Modernist Myths* (Cambridge, MA: MIT Press, 1985), 55.

188

Index

Page numbers in boldface indicate illustrations.

191